D0611490

Stories from Novice Teachers

This Is Induction?

Lisa Scherff
Mike Daria

UNIVERSITY PRESS OF AMERICA,® INC.
Lanham • Boulder • New York • Toronto • Plymouth, UK

educa
WISSER MEMORIAL LIBRARY

LB 1731.4
.S34
2010
c.1

Copyright © 2010 by
University Press of America,® Inc.
4501 Forbes Boulevard
Suite 200
Lanham, Maryland 20706
UPA Acquisitions Department (301) 459-3366

Estover Road
Plymouth PL6 7PY
United Kingdom

All rights reserved
Printed in the United States of America
British Library Cataloging in Publication Information Available

Library of Congress Control Number: 2010921178
ISBN: 978-0-7618-5085-4 (paperback : alk. paper)
eISBN: 978-0-7618-5086-1

∞ ™ The paper used in this publication meets the minimum
requirements of American National Standard for Information
Sciences—Permanence of Paper for Printed Library Materials,
ANSI/NISO Z39.48-1992.

We dedicate this book to the teachers who let us tell their stories . . . and to the millions of teachers who work so hard each day in our nation's schools.
—Lisa and Mike

Contents

Foreword: Why We Must Support New Teachers

Barnett Berry

Center for Teaching Quality
Hillsborough, North Carolina

I often wonder why America's education system is so willing to "eat its young." New teachers are often assigned the most difficult subjects and the most challenging, diverse students in the highest-need schools. Then, they are rarely supported in their first years on the job—despite the fact that when novices are "formally inducted," they are 2–3 times more likely to remain in the classroom. Indeed, few states and districts offer the kind of comprehensive support new teachers need and deserve. In fact, researchers have found that only one percent of beginning teachers nationally are receiving comprehensive induction programs (Smith & Ingersoll, 2004). As a result over 30% of new teachers leave within the first five years of teaching, and over 50% of novices who teach in urban schools leave within the first *three* years (National Commission on Teaching and America's Future, 2003). Indeed, most new-teacher induction programs in America's public schools are under-conceptualized, under-developed, under-supported, and under-funded.

Granted, over the last ten years the proportion of novices receiving induction support rose from 41% in 1990 to almost 79% in 2000 (Smith & Ingersoll, 2004). Only 17 states actually mandate and fund induction programs, leaving many new teachers largely on their own to "sink or swim." Some states require induction programs, but may invest less than $100 per new teacher. Some analysts have estimated the cost of high quality induction programs at $6000 per new teacher (Center for Teaching Quality, 2006). This figure might seem expensive. But consider what it costs when new teacher investments are not made. With teacher turnover is "spiraling out of control," analysts have estimated that the nation spends more than $7 billion a year to replace teachers who leave. Some districts like Chicago lose 4800 teachers a year at the cost of almost $18,000—amounting to a staggering $86 million a year (Barnes & Crowe, 2007).

Even when programs are in place, mentors are not available and trained. A recent Center for Teaching Quality working conditions survey in Arizona found that only three out of five new teachers had a formal mentor assigned to them, of those who received support indicated the "help" provided as "critical." Only 60% of the novices indicated their mentor taught the same content they do in the same did and over 50% had never observed their mentor teach. Only 40% reported that they actually had at least weekly discussions with their mentor about their teaching. Over 25% reported their discussions took place only monthly (Berry, Fuller, & Williams, 2007).

Yet, despite the growing evidence on the relationship between induction programs and new teacher retention and student achievement, most states and school districts do far too little for its novices. If America had deliberately set out to create a highly dysfunctional system of new teacher support, we could not have done a better job. Teachers, even those who are prepared need sound induction support. The 2005 MetLife survey found that many teachers felt *ill-prepared* during their first year to deal with critical aspects of their jobs—working with children of varying abilities, getting the support they needed from their principal, and obtaining the resources and supplies necessary to teach effectively (MetLife, 2007). Our own new teacher studies at the Center for Teaching Quality reveal that many novices enter classrooms not knowing enough about how to find and design relevant and engaging lessons, develop and score valid and reliable tests, teach content to students who read well below grade level, and work effectively with second language learners.

In addition, more teachers are entering classrooms without hardly any preparation at all. Almost one in three teachers enter teaching through shortcut alternative certification routes, with only a few weeks of much-needed pedagogical coursework before they are assigned to some of the most challenging schools and students. A recent report by the Public Agenda Foundation revealed that only 38% of "high quality" alternative certification recruits rated their preparation in *helping struggling students* as excellent or good. Only 49% claimed they were prepared to provide individualized instruction to their students. Other studies show that they are less likely to be effective in raising student achievement than their traditionally prepared counterparts.

High quality new teacher induction programs:

• Pair new teachers with trained mentors in similar grades and subject areas;
• Reduce novices' workloads and structure teaching schedules to provide common planning time and frequent face-to-face interaction among mentors and novices;

- Provide release time for both the mentor and novice for observations and analysis;
- Offer ongoing professional development relevant to the needs of novice teachers and give them access to an external network of beginning teachers; and
- Develop a standards-based formal assessment of beginning teachers and the induction program itself (Ingersoll & Kralik, 2004).

One can find high-quality new teacher induction elements somewhere in America—but just not in one place. For example, New Teacher Center at the University of California-Santa Cruz knows how to train mentors and use standards-based protocol to assist novices. Stanford University and Connecticut's Beginning Educator Support and Training (*BEST*) Program have created valid and reliable new teacher assessments. The Center for Teaching Quality is using new virtual tools to spread the expertise of National Board Certified Teachers to novices in high needs schools. No one state or district has put all the pieces together.

The kind of induction and new teacher supports needed are readily found in other nations and professions. In Japan, induction for new teachers lasts one year and includes weekly training both in and out of school. To lighten new teachers' workloads, accommodate their heavy training schedule, and allow release time for extensive mentoring, the program assigns one part-time experienced teacher to each new teacher or one full-time teacher for two new teachers. Other professions in the United States invest in their novices at much higher levels than education does. Before they practice independently, aspiring architects work under the tutelage of an approved, expert practitioner for three years before earning a license, and law firms do not send their novice lawyer, fresh out of school, to present arguments in their most important cases. Yet in teaching we make few policy distinctions between the very new and the very experienced professional. It defies common sense. Prepared and supported new teachers will remain in teaching longer and teach more effectively. Why is so hard to invest in teaching—the profession that makes all others possible?

NOTE

A recent study by the New Teacher Center has estimated that for every $1 spent on a high-quality teacher induction program, a return of $1.66 is seen in just five years in terms of enhanced student learning and reduced teacher turnover costs.

REFERENCES

Barnes, G., & Crowe, E. (2007). *The Costs of Teacher Turnover.* Washington DC: NCTAF.

Berry, B., Fuller, E., & Williams, A. (2007). *Steming the Tide of Teacher Attrition.* Hillsborough, NC: Center for Teaching Quality.

Center for Teaching Quality (2006). http://www.teachingquality.org/whytqmatters/induction.htm

Ingersoll, R., & Kralik, J. M. (2004, February). *The Impact of Mentoring on Teacher Retention: What the Research Says.* Denver: Education Commission of the States. http://www.ecs.org/clearinghouse/50/36/5036.htm

MetLife (2005). *The American Teacher: Transitions and the Role of Supportive Relationships.* New York: Author. http://www.metlife.com/WPSAssets/34996838801118758796V1FATS_2004.pdf

National Commission on Teaching and America's Future (2003). *No Dream Denied.* Washington: Author.

Smith, T., & Ingersoll, R. (2004). What are the Effects of Induction and Mentoring on Beginning Teacher Turnover? *American Educational Research Journal, 41,* 681–714.

Introduction

There is so much out there that could cause a teacher to quit these days. The red tape, the amount of work you have to do that solves no problems whatsoever, nasty coworkers, poor administration, no in school support, no one explains anything to you, constant changes that make more work and don't fix anything, no parent support, no student support, arrogant cruel students, violent students, apathetic students who tell you everything you do is worthless and the class agrees because they think they can get out of a test that way, parents who you never hear from until their child fails and though they always fail—this time it is clearly your fault, low pay, 15 hour days when you are done with everything, in-services that don't help, faculty meetings that take your time and don't help, then dishes, laundry, family and you—the things neglected for this other stuff—these are many but not all of the reasons to quit teaching. The good news is—look at this list—it is so ridiculous that it is funny. That is how I don't quit. There is so much that sucks about teaching—it doesn't even matter anymore. I teach because kids need a positive role model and even though they may be nasty and not appreciate it—they are still exposed to a positive role model. I teach because English is forever and it is about people—even if they don't want to—students might just learn something that makes a difference. Because truly changing kids is always a possibility—all this other stuff is just a joke that doesn't even matter. It helps me keep perspective about how important my job is—look what they are trying to do to educating youth. Look what youth and the family have become. I am needed in the schools—someone who can take it has got to expose these kids to something good and positive—even if they don't want it—they still need the chance to get it.

The e-mail excerpt above from a novice teacher delineates many of the reasons why there is a teacher shortage: red tape, antagonistic colleagues, pressure from parents, low pay, and ineffective in-service and professional development. While some aspects of teaching, like low salaries, cannot be fixed by school principals, mentors, and colleagues, several others can be addressed and possibly fixed by those same stakeholders.

Novice teachers often cite their first years in the classroom as unsupportive and lonely. Feelings of isolation and being overwhelmed help contribute to the substantial numbers of teachers leaving the profession. In fact, 25–35% of beginning teachers do not stay in the classroom more than two or three years (Darling-Hammond, 2006; Gold, 1996) and nearly 50% of all teachers will quit within the first five years (Ingersoll, 2003). The initial year in the classroom is a crucial part of a teacher's career with long term implications for job satisfaction and career length (Darling-Hammond, 2006; Feiman-Nemser, 1983; Hebert & Worthy, 2001; Johnson, et al., 2004; Lortie, 1975; McDonald, 1980; Scherff, 2008). Most beginning teachers leave the profession displeased because of low salaries, student discipline problems, lack of support, poor working conditions, inadequate preparation, and insufficient opportunities to participate in decision making (e.g., Andrews & Martin, 2003; Cochran-Smith, 2004; Darling-Hammond, 2003; Hirsch, 2006; Ingersoll, 2003, 2004; Kent, 2000; Liu & Meyer, 2005; Rogers & Babinski, 1999; Veenman, 1984).

Because today's work environment offers multiple career possibilities, jobs with higher status and pay, more productive work environments, and better chances for promotion to high levels, prospective teachers may not necessarily choose teaching (Johnson & Birkeland, 2003). Others leave teaching because they did not intend to stay in the profession long-term. "Serial careers are the norm, and short-term employment is common" (Johnson & Birkeland, 2003, p. 585). Another more recent cause for teacher attrition is the accountability associated with the No Child Left Behind Act (2001). In a recent study, over 55% of those surveyed indicated an "overemphasis on testing" as a reason as influencing their decision to leave the profession (Hirsch, 2006, p. 8). Additionally, Sunderman, Tracey, Kim, and Orfield found that "many of the teachers in schools that were identified as needing improvement do not plan to be teaching in them five years in the future . . . [and] also believed that the NCLB sanctions would cause teachers to transfer out of schools not making adequate progress" (2004, p. 3).

BACKGROUND

Stories from Novice Teachers: This is Induction? began as a deliberate effort by twelve first-year high school teachers and me (Lisa) during the summer of 2004. At that time, I took a leave of absence from my university position to return to return to high school teaching in my home state. The teachers featured in this book, all former students in the teacher education program, chose to create an e-mail listserv with me so that we could maintain contact and form a support group. From the beginning, we determined that our online communication should extend beyond our circle and be used to inform the educational community. The teachers wanted their experiences to assist other new teachers as they transitioned from student teacher/intern to "real" teacher.

Very quickly into our e-mail dialogue, I realized there were mountainous issues faced by the new teachers—including myself—that we were not prepared for. Some of us lacked the necessary technology to complete required paperwork; others were left to fend for themselves amidst a sea of unawareness; still, others taught overcrowded classes with few resources. It is because of these issues, and the fact that research consistently tells us *this* is not the way to induct, mentor, and retain new teachers that we are committed to this project and believe that teachers' stories can impact change.

We began e-mailing in July 2004 and, though the participation dropped off as some left the profession and others got married or started families, we still use the listserv to talk to each other occasionally. The greatest activity was during the 2004–2005 school year when we posted a total of 607 messages. Since we began our collaborative journey (and at the time this book was formally begun), four left the profession, two left and returned, and the remaining six were still teaching, although two had changed schools. For myself, returning to the high school classroom did not go as planned—instead of one year's leave—I was back at the university at the end of the fall semester. Because so many of us became the statistics we had read about, we felt we had an even greater story to tell.

In the fall of 2005 I moved to Alabama and, though I kept up with the e-mails, we nearly abandoned the idea of writing a book. However, troubling circumstances surrounding one teacher's decision to leave the profession prompted us to continue. In addition, I had the opportunity to work with one of our students—Mary Beasley—who had recently finished her undergraduate degree and returned to begin her graduate work. She began reading the e-mail transcripts and once I heard her comments and questions, from the important perspective of a new teacher, and one who is not familiar with the teachers featured in the book, I knew we had to go forward.

In April 2007, after encouragement to continue writing, I added the much needed administrative perspective and invited Mike Daria to collaborate. Mike is a former classroom teacher and middle school principal, who recently earned his doctorate in educational leadership and is the Executive Director of Personnel for the Tuscaloosa City Schools. With his help and insight, the book really took shape and we now have a text that can be used in schools and district offices with administrators and teachers, and in colleges of education with graduate students in educational leadership programs.

Our fear is that with the multitude of induction and mentoring books and programs out there busy administrators will resort to letting someone else do it, whether that someone is a series of checklists and rubrics or "outside experts." From our own experience as classroom teachers, mentors and supervisors, teacher educators, and through completing many readings in our own graduate programs, we know that it is easy to go to with what looks a simple program. It is our hope that the real-life experiences of novice teachers featured in this book will promote discussion among and between school principals, principals in training, and even district-level superintendents and administrators.

Our main goal in writing this book is to use the novices' stories to inform school principals and district-level administrators of the situations that promote or hinder new teacher growth so that we can lower attrition rates and foster student achievement. To do this, we have organized the book as follows. Each chapter focuses on a particular novice teacher induction/mentoring issue and follows a similar format: a summary of the teachers' stories told using e-mail and/or interview excerpts and separate commentaries and questions posed by me and Mike. Our hope is that each teacher's story becomes analogous to a case to study for readers. However, these are not fabricated cases, written by "experts"; they are the teachers' actual struggles chronicled through the conversations and discussions among the group. Thus, they are not always neat and tidy—much like real teaching in real schools. Finally, in the Epilogue, teachers who felt comfortable doing so provide their own follow-up tales with insights and lessons learned.

Most of the "how to" books currently on the market are written by professors in educational leadership programs or consultants who used to be in education. Their strengths are that they have up-to-date research and draw from successful programs to provide assistance to administrators. However, their ease of use is precisely what we know from experience can be the pitfalls of using them: checklists, rubrics, and lists of what to do become "programs" and "requirements" and seem like quick-fixes to problems.

HOW TO USE THIS BOOK

Our book serves as a learning tool in multiple ways and for multiple readers. Pre-service teachers might use this book as part of their methods block to discuss critical events before they become first year teachers. Principals could use this book as part of a book study for new teachers or for their own growth as leaders. The book also could be read and discussed by high school departments that are having internal conflicts.

The greatest feature of the book is that the cases are real. In many of the texts that we come across, the narratives presented do not read like actual events that teachers face. Mike and I are not outside researchers or consultants that are writing about what occurs in schools; he and I have only recently left the classroom and in our current roles work very closely with pre-service and in-service teachers. Another asset is that we incorporate several voices and perspectives. We find that most induction and mentoring books are written from one role to another (researcher to principal or university professor to teacher). Our book is for many readers—teacher educators, administrators, teachers, prospective teachers, department heads, researchers—and is crafted and informed by several perspectives—novice teacher, experienced teacher, teacher educator, university instructor, principal, and district-level administrator. Each reader can use the book for specific purposes:

- in a teacher education program to learn about the realities of the first year(s) and how to deal with problematic situations they might encounter;
- in educational administration or educational leadership courses to learn how to create healthier school cultures and support/retain novice and veteran teachers;
- as a supplemental text in a school-based, district-based, or state-based induction and/or mentoring program to inform participants;
- as part of a principal induction program to help school leaders as they transition from teacher to administrator;
- in in-service workshops as part of continuing professional development for teachers and administrators; and
- in a departmental, school, or other book study group to learn to how work through similar issues in their own schools.

THE TEACHERS

We think it is key that we provide some background information on the teachers whose experiences were turned into the cases for this book. All of the teachers held a bachelor's degree in their content area (or the equivalent number of related hours). They then completed a 36 hour master of science degree program that included a year-long internship in a high school (where they taught 90-minute blocks each semester); they conducted an action research project in their classroom; they took coursework in language arts methods, reading in the content areas, and professional development; and, they completed a 16 hour education minor, with courses such as educational psychology, technology, special education, and cultural studies to finalize their certification process.

None of the teachers we feature talked about their coursework being too theoretical and not practical enough. All said they felt very well prepared to enter the profession. While some of their issues might parallel those of non-certified teachers, or those who came from alternative programs, we feel that presenting their stories as cases for study is unique, and important, in that they all agreed that they were very well prepared for teaching. What they were not prepared for were compromising their principles; dumbing down the curriculum for students; promoting/giving students grades who don't deserve it because of parental pressure; cold and uncaring colleagues; ineffective administrators; principals catering to parents; administrators ignoring their teachers and staff; and feeling unappreciated most of the time. Data on each of the teachers, as well as information concerning their internship placement and employment status (as of 2008) is provided in Table 1.

Table 1. Participants, Type of Placement/First Paid Position, and Employment Status

Name	Internship Placement (TN) (2003-2004)	First Paid Position (2004-2005)	Year 1 Status (2004-2005)	Year 2 Status (2005-2006)	Year 3 Status (2006-2007)	Year 4 Status (2007-2008)
Nicole*	Rural/Suburban	Urban (GA)	Taught 9/04 - 12/04	Suburban (GA)	Not teaching	Not teaching
Lisa	Suburban	Rural (TN)	⟶		Not teaching	Business sector
Toni	Suburban/Urban	Suburban (TN)	⟶	Left teaching 12/05	Working in family business	Family business
Rachel*	Rural	Urban (GA)	Left teaching 06/05	Not-for-profit work	Returned to teaching (TN)	Teaching (TN)
Lane	Rural	Suburban (TN)	⟶		Left and returned (TN)	Teaching (TN)
Erin	Rural	Rural, Suburban/Urban (TN)	Long-term substitute	Juvenile detention teacher (GA)	Still teaching (GA)	⟶
Jennifer	Rural	Suburban (NC)	⟶			
Shawn	Suburban	Suburban (AL)		Let go 10/05	Law enforcement	
Kasey**	Urban	Urban (FL)	⟶	Suburban (TN)	⟶	
Kathleen***	Rural	Rural (TN)	⟶		Maternity leave	Stay at home mother
Dan**	Rural	Urban (FL)	⟶	Rural (TN)	⟶	
Susan	Suburban/Urban	Suburban (GA)	⟶			

* Both teachers were employed at the same school;
** Both teachers were employed at the same school;
*** Kathleen's first job was at her internship site.

TEACHER STORIES AS CASES

The use of narratives in teacher research has become progressively more recognized and influential (see, for example, Alsup, 2006; Ayers, 2001; Connelly & Clandinin, 1999; Craig, 2003; Danielewicz, 2001). Teacher stories, like traditional tales we are familiar with, include characters and a plot that develops over time (Brockmeier & Harré, 1997).With story creation using mechanisms such as online communication (e-mails, blogs, etc.), the stories can be solely or mutually constructed. Stories created online provide both a frame of reference for others (an experiencing of the same or similar event) and a glimpse into a unique world (each person is working in and experiencing a distinctive culture and world), transforming a support network into a knowledge community (Scherff, 2008). Knowledge communities are "safe, story-telling places where people narrate the rawness of their experiences, negotiate meaning for such experiences, and authorize their own and others' narrative interpretations of situations as legitimate . . . teachers validate and consolidate their experiences both as individuals and as members of a professional community" (Craig, 2000, p. 15).

Teacher stories provide teachers and administrators a method to reflect on and learn from their beliefs, values, instructional practices, and professional environment (Connelly & Clandinin, 1990; Rushton, 2004). Brockmeier and Harré (1997) suggest "it is above all through narrative that we make sense of the wider, more differentiated, and more complex texts and contexts of our experience" (p. 264). As such, teachers' stories are significant theoretical and practical tools for teacher education programs, teacher educators, administrators, and other teachers (Alsup, 2006; Bullough & Baugham, 1996; Connelly & Clandinin, 1990, 1999; Estola, 2003).

A FINAL WORD

Although our book features English teachers, the "English" part of their story is not our primary focus; what is most interesting is that teaching English was rarely the problem, but navigating the schools and working with colleagues and administrators was. Thus, we believe our text's range is far greater than many of the induction and case books we have read. Our book can be used across content areas in teacher education programs, in educational leadership classes, in schools and school districts, and in state departments of education.

We must offer a word of caution concerning objectivity, however. As with all stories, they are written from one perspective, and from one's position, both physical and emotional. We do not deny that the teachers' (and our) experiences are colored and impacted by our pasts, our beliefs and values, and our teaching philosophies. Nonetheless, we believe in and stand by our tales and suggestions for teachers, teacher educators, principals, and other administrators.

NOTE

Some teachers requested pseudonyms be utilized; pseudonyms are used for all schools and names of colleagues and administrators.

Chapter One

Induction and Mentoring

As a "new teacher" three times in my teaching career, I (Lisa) experienced different forms of mentoring and induction with each position. With my first job (1996) in Southwest Florida, I actually arrived two days after school started, so I missed whatever school-based induction activities were offered to faculty. However, I worked for a supportive principal (who had been my assistant principal in high school) and department chair (who had been my ninth grade English teacher), so I was unofficially mentored and supported throughout those first few years. The district offered multiple chances for teachers to earn professional development hours, and I remember attending training in areas such as discipline and critical thinking and actually getting stipends to do so.

My second and third positions were very different in terms of both how the school and district inducted and mentored me. With my second job (1999), I do not remember much, to be honest. That is not to say that nothing was done—I just do not recall anything. I know for sure that none of us new (i.e., new to the school and district) teachers had any formal mentoring. Again, I found induction through district-level activities—including training to have a student teacher under my care. However, I had to seek those opportunities out.

My last high school teaching adventure actually took place in the fall of 2004, when I was on leave from my university position. This last experience, ironically, was the only one in which there appeared to be some sort of "formal" induction and mentoring. Nonetheless, appearances can be unreliable, as I quickly learned. I was razzled and dazzled by nice canvas bags with tons of goodies and classroom supplies. I was excited to hear that I would have a mentor and buddy to get me through the first year. Yet, everything "promised" ended the second the students arrived on day one. I was left alone, with few answers and even less assistance. I learned a very valuable lesson: looks can be deceiving, as the excerpt from an August email shows. *I have to do a "new teacher" portfolio, even though I did one the first year I taught. Neither my dept head, "mentor," and "buddy" have stopped by my room once. Thank God I have not needed any of them.*

My third time as a new teacher, although admittedly only at one school, shocked me in terms of the types of mentoring and induction available to and/or forced on novice teachers and experienced teachers who were new to a school, district, or state. I remained just one semester. It is with this still fresh in my mind that we have our first case chapter concerning induction and mentoring overall.

There are various types of "new" teachers: beginning teachers directly out of undergraduate teacher education programs, adults who begin teaching after raising families, career changers, and experienced teachers who change schools (Brock & Grady, 2001). Because each of these new teachers has a different level of experience working in schools, and dealing with colleagues and administrators, their induction and mentoring needs are different. Many induction and mentoring programs fail because they do not take these differences into account.

Teacher induction programs are not extra training, but are planned experiences for teachers who have already completed basic preparation. Induction programs are considered a bridge, enabling the "student of teaching" to become a "teacher of students" (Smith & Ingersoll, 2004, p. 683). However, the intensity and scope of induction programs differ widely. Induction can range from a one-day orientation session held before the start of the school year to a series of activities and meetings lasting several years. Some induction programs are school-based, while others are state-adopted and/or mandated. While some programs have minimal requirements, others involve new teachers completing workshops (technology, discipline, etc.), creating portfolios, taking part in online discussions, and attending district-based meetings at the same time they are navigating the first year in the classroom (Scherff, 2008).

Mentoring, personal support for novices from expert teachers/peers, is one aspect of induction. As with induction programs, mentoring can look different from school to school and district to district. At minimum, some principals merely assign mentors to new teachers, with no guidelines for their responsibilities. In other cases, mentors are assigned, but hesitant or unwilling to take on that role. Still, there are recommendations for effective mentoring: structured programs, mentor training, release time for mentors, common planning time with novices, etc. (Darling-Hammond, 2003; Feiman-Nemser,

1996; Holloway, 2001). Effective mentoring combines the professional—observing, evaluating, advising—and the personal—befriending and counseling (Rippon & Martin, 2006). These conditions are critical for mentoring programs to have the desired positive impact. As Linda Darling-Hammond (2006) notes, expert mentors are the component of induction with the "greatest effect on teacher retention and learning" (p. 340).

For the novice teachers we studied, mentoring and induction were analogous to the classic children's tale "Goldilocks and the Three Bears" in that it rarely fit their needs. As the following cases show, there were several instances of too much induction and mentoring and with others of not enough; rarely was anything just right or the right kind. We begin this chapter with novice teachers' experiences with induction. In Case #1, we focus on Dan and Kasey's stories of disproportionate induction activities which could potentially occur in districts that do not coordinate their efforts with those of the state. When both novices accepted teaching positions at the same high school in Florida, they had to go through two concurrent induction programs, one at the state-level and the other at the district-level. Neither program would accept relevant (or even nearly identical) work they completed in graduate school, such as the electronic portfolio. So, both had to repeat many things they already knew how to do for the sake the induction programs. Because they spent time on two sets of overlapping induction activities, they had less time to prepare for and teach their classes. Lane, in Case #2, had similar experiences, although she only had one induction program to participate in.

While Dan, Kasey, and Lane experienced too much or counterproductive induction and mentoring, the rest of the group (in Case #3) encountered what we call traditional induction programs—those organized sessions that orient new teachers to rules, policies, and procedures. While most of the programs were designed to provide helpful information and set up peer mentoring, that was rarely accomplished. Moreover, these "induction" sessions were sometimes woefully inadequate for what the beginning teachers needed and wanted. Case #3 shows that while a general orientation to the school and district is necessary and valuable, it has to be planned and implemented with new teachers' needs in mind. Likewise, if schools are going to assign mentors, they need to feel a sense of responsibility to the process of assisting new teachers in order for mentoring to truly work.

In Case #4, we shift to the teachers who received no official/formal induction or mentoring of any kind: Shawn, Kathleen, Nicole, and Erin. Each had to create and find his or her own ways to be inducted and mentored. While Shawn's school did not offer a formal mentoring program, he was lucky to have helpful colleagues. Kathleen's story is similar; her school did not offer formal mentoring, but she had the benefit of completing her internship there the year prior. Thus, she knew everyone in her department. Nicole and Erin's stories offer interesting points for department chairs and administrators: we cannot forget about new teachers who come to schools several weeks into a school year or are interim teachers. They need induction and mentoring just like "regular" new teachers.

CASE #1: WASTEFUL DUPLICATION

While new teachers often do not have proper mentoring and support, the two teachers in this case are inundated with forms of support. Adult learning must be applicable and individualized in order for it to be effective. However, with Dan and Kasey it seems as though good intentions have resulted in the structures and mechanisms of mentoring and induction without the intended results. In fact, the structures in place work counterproductively for these two new teachers and seemingly contribute to their exit from the system.

The greatest concern with these teachers is clearly identified by Dan who states, "The main problem with the whole system is that new teachers have enough to learn and deal with as it is, and it seems that all they have done is give us extra busy work." When schools and systems implement mentoring and induction plans, they must pay attention to the needs of the adult learner. While the emphasis on technology and dialogue are commendable in the program, there seems to be more of a focus on documentation that support has taken place instead of the actual support. Mentoring is about relationships. Dan and Kasey do not express any notion of an individual guiding them through their first year, assisting them with the procedures of the local school, and coaching them in instructional strategies in their classrooms. Dan expresses an interest in engaging in dialogue with peers at his school, but is opposed to traveling across town to meet with individuals whom he does not know or see enough to engage in meaningful and honest conversation. He writes,

The fact that as a "First Year Teacher," even though I've already taught, I have to go to a website set up by the county and report to a discussion board much like this one only far less rewarding or comforting because I'm conversing with teachers I've never met and have no bond with, is absurd. Not only that, I'm assigned some administrator teacher who puts "assignments" on the board for us to read and respond to; I've already done this, and in a much more effective way. It's insulting, because I feel like I'm being watched. The discussion board would be a good idea, if it wasn't mandated, my job didn't depend on it, and I wasn't babysat by someone.

The District Induction Program

The district itself required all first year (first year in Florida) teachers attend a 4 day [introductory] conference. Fortunately, I was still finishing graduate courses, so I missed this part. However, from what I understand, it was nothing more than a long series of painful lectures and conferences. At least one of which introduced teachers to a new program they would be required to participate in called Teachscape. Teachscape is sort of an online course for first year teachers. It offers help to teachers for gaining new ideas, or in the case of teachers with Masters degrees, rehashing the ones they have been discussing for two or three years. Each teacher is assigned to a discussion group that meets three or four times a semester and is required to turn in a series of what I have yet to discover to be useful assignments. Of course, I am speaking rather cynically, but then, why shouldn't I when on a weekly basis I am required to do an excessive amount of extra work that is very similar to things I had to do to get my Masters. This idea could actually be more helpful to new teachers without education degrees. But teachers who have taught for several years in other states are also required to take part in this. New teachers have enough to learn and deal with, and all they have done is give us extra busy work. Well, thanks, but I don't need any busy work.

Complications with the Induction System

It took the district a month and a half to get me an employee number and even acknowledge the fact that I existed as a teacher in their system. It took them another month to put me in a Teachscape group. They neglected to notice the fact that they set me up in a group for middle school teachers. This, of course, is certainly a problem since I do not teach middle school and if I participated in the wrong program, I would have to do the whole thing all over again once they figured it out. Once they got me in the right system, the stupid online thing did not allow me access. It was November before I had even gotten started and ⅔ of my assignments were late. That was simply my induction to the district.

The School Induction Program

As far as my induction to the school, that was a little better, though after the week of first year teacher stuff, we spent another week of in-service meetings for the school. None of these days devoted time to getting rooms ready, getting acquainted with curriculum or anything important like that. We went to some retreat place and had a very tasty breakfast and spent the day coming up with a "Mission Statement," among other things. However, the school did have a wonderful moment when we were introduced to every teacher in the school. Much the way a church introduces its new members, the new teachers stood in a line while the other teachers came through and shook our hands. The whole process took almost an hour with the number of new teachers and resident teachers as well. I felt quite welcome after that.

We were assigned a peer teacher and a "buddy," of which the "buddy" teacher was later retracted. GO figure that one. The peer teacher is responsible for helping you do things, learn "the ropes," and all the paperwork. I think I've seen mine twice. While I like my peer teacher, it has been difficult for us to find the time to get together. Actually, I like him because he doesn't breathe down my neck; he simply offers to be there if I need anything. Of course, being one who rarely asks for help even when I need it kind of defeats the purpose in this case.

At the end of the school year, Dan reflected on how the two concurrent induction and mentoring programs added to the stress of being a new teacher.

In Teachscape we have a little class and there are about five or six of us. We meet with a mentor teacher once a month or every couple of months. They are allotted an hour and half to two hour classes and we sit and talk. Part of the problem was I had to drive all the way across the county. It takes 30 to 40 minutes to get there and when I get there, I just sit there and listen to her talk about some particular teaching strategy or about Teachscape and how you use it. It got to be ridiculous. I could do this on the telephone or over e-mail. We had to do that first semester and then second semester was a whole second course. We got inservice credit but, it was just too much. It wasn't too much work as much as it was just stress. It was like, I gotta do this and this and this and this and this and on top of that I have to do this and this means I have to do this this this this and this.

And we had GEMS, their other induction program. We were supposed to develop an electronic portfolio but we couldn't use the one that we had [done in the teacher education program] because they have one set up online. You had to fill in everything there . . . it seemed like every week something new came up and something was added to stuff that we had to do or take care of or the meetings that we had to be in.

Kasey, who moved to Florida at the same time and also taught at the same school, echoed Dan's frustration over the double induction experience.

I don't know how it is in Florida or what the internship is, but it was irritating being from Tennessee. I already did the electronic portfolio. I already took the classes. You come down here and it's like you've gotta do the same thing over again. You have GEMS (peer teacher stuff) and they observe you and then you're supposed to do an electronic portfolio. Then you have Teachscape; you meet with a group and depending on your group leader you have a whole lot of work or you don't; you look at these videos then you write reactions, just like an education class. At the first meeting they said, "You know, well if you leave the county we don't want you to leave because you said you didn't have enough help or you didn't have enough support."

The idea behind it was to give you as much support as possible. I think the GEMS things or the peer teacher was a good idea, but Teachscape and putting it all on you when you're a first year teacher when you're trying to figure out the best way to grade, how to deal with your students, some kind of schedule, is too much. There should be some kind of induction, but they should structure it over a couple of years instead; they're trying to help but they're not. What they're really doing is loading on more work for you to do, especially when you're trying to just stay afloat your first year.

CASE #2: INDUCTION OR BRAINWASHING?

Lane's experiences appear to come from a school system with an established culture that it desires to continue. While it is important to transfer the mission, vision, goal, and objectives to new teachers, it should not be done so in an intimidating or forceful manner. One negative consequence to this type of induction program is that it is not welcoming to new teachers. It sends them the message that they are visitors only and will not be contributing members of the school or system until they conform. To beginning teachers with new strategies and skill sets, this can be a major disappointment. As Case #2 shows, the fact that Lane had taken a three-hour technology class and completed an electronic portfolio during her teacher preparation program did not exempt her from having to repeat the activities all over again—at the same time she was beginning her first job. Yet, ironically, teachers who had been in the district for years were excused from having to learn the latest technology. Lane offered her induction story a few days after the school year began.

I just finished my two days of new teacher orientation . . . [I was] sooo bored. I complained and stressed all year, it was so worth it. I came into this completely prepared. Our new teacher orientation was more of a brainwashing. We spent two days going through "sessions" which educated us on the "Watson Way" of doing things. They wanted to make sure that we do things their way, and I have bags, pencils, mugs, etc. to prove it and remind me. I really didn't find it at all helpful except to provide me with a list of jargon and buzz words that have helped me survive in the county: Schlecty, Working on the Work, Critical Friends, Design Qualities . . . always good to keep those handy to throw into conversation when needed.

In addition to all this [and] the one thing that really pissed me off, though, is that all new teachers are required to take a 12 hour standards-based technology class, complete a huge final project, and present it at the last meeting, proving that we have met the standards and requirements necessary to stay—and here I thought my Masters degree would suffice. I can comp out of it as long as I show the lady my digital portfolio, the [university] syllabus, and my transcripts.

Faulty Logic?

Even though Lane sent the required documentation to the school district and showed them her electronic portfolio, she was required to take the class. She later wrote,

> And the county made me take the technology class—all stinking twelve hours, a final project, and presentation, because first-year teachers have plenty of free time for that! This in itself has been a blessing and a pain in the ass, as I have come out of it with a website, but also five less evenings of spare time. Now explain the logic of this to me. You are going to require every new teacher to take twelve hours of technology classes along with a presentation and project; however, all veteran teachers are exempt if they have been in the county for over three years. It seems to me that anyone who completes a college or graduate level education program is required to demonstrate a certain amount of competency when it comes to technology, unless you attended the "Backwoods Center for Edumacation," and consequently would not be hired by this county in the first place. And yet the old, deaf teacher who graduated from college before the Civil Rights Movement can still continue his or her teaching without meeting any technology requirements. Can new teachers get a break?

CASE #3: MORE OF THE SAME

The individual stories featured in this case reinforce the notion that while many different entities talk about induction and mentoring, and how it should look, many times it is just that—talk. Traditional induction and mentoring in some schools seems to be nothing more than saying "here is your mentor" or "come to this after-school mentoring session." New teachers need more than that. They also need mentors who are invested in helping beginning teachers reach their full potential. At the other end, mentors need to be compensated somehow for their role in the partnership, whether through course release or paid compensation. Mentors need to be carefully screened and selected, not just named. Finally, mentors need to want to guide new teachers.

Lisa's sentiment is one that is heard too often. She appears to be a dedicated educator, who in order to maintain focus, relegates herself to the four walls of her classroom focusing on her assigned students. Lisa appears willing and excited to contribute to the school as a whole, but unfortunately is not provided the opportunity or invitation to do so. Within a short period of time she realizes that the formal support systems are on paper only and do not truly exist. Lisa's past experiences allow her to have a comparison, and she underscores the importance of collegial support. She references her business experiences where peers all work to invite and welcome new employees. Lisa quickly finds that her school formally employs support systems but does not have a true culture of support. Too often teachers assume it is someone else's responsibility to induct new teachers be it a mentor, the system program, or the principal. In reality, schools should support cultures where it is the professional obligation of all to induct and support new teachers.

Rachael's case is similar to Lisa's in that she has identified that the mentoring system is nothing more than a form of documentation. The spirit of the mentoring system does not exist. Rachael's case identifies one of the great complexities in mentoring, especially with the large number of new teachers and the smaller number of experienced teachers. Identifying mentors is a difficult process and decision. Schools must commit to assigning mentors who are dedicated and passionate about the purpose of mentoring. Too often, mentors are selected based on their room location, preparation period, or veteran status in the school. These are not always the best criteria for mentor selection and pairing. How different Rachael's case may have been had she experienced positive mentoring with a peer to assist her growth as a new teacher.

Jennifer, much like Lisa, sees the mentoring much like a contrived professional relationship. Mentors should be trained. The mentor in Jennifer's case appears to assert her status as a veteran teacher rather than her assistance as a helpful guide. New teachers, while often willing to learn from experienced teachers, may not be receptive to directives instead of support. Another negative consequence in this relationship that Jennifer identifies is the connection that the mentor has to the principal. Mentors should have no connection to the supervision and evaluation process. It may be assumed that Jennifer will not be able to confide in her mentor with the knowledge that the information or discussions may find their way to the principal's office.

Lisa

We had a one-day introduction by the school board where we were told how to sign up for a computer account, how not to get sued by following all of the special education laws, etc. I haven't been sued yet, so I suppose the training was good (I'm teaching irony right now in case you haven't noticed). Seriously, I believe that I was assigned a mentor; however, my mentor teacher is too busy with her own schedule to help me. Don't get me wrong; she's great and answers all of my questions. However, I'm learning as I go and from my mistakes. As far as all the paperwork and everything that we have to do, I really haven't had a mentoring teacher, which I didn't think was going to be the case here.

It bothered me for a long time. Then I just learned: I'm here for the kids. I'm going to do my own thing. If I'm not part of the group it's okay; I'm not in high school anymore. I didn't experience that working in business, so that's been a big adjustment. Every company I ever worked for, any time a new person came on board they were made to feel welcome. People would ask them out to lunch. Everybody.

I think that they need to have mentoring programs in place. Establish them, not just say "she's just going to be your mentor," but have established programs in place, so that they learn the ropes, especially somebody they can really talk to, somebody who can give them a pep talk when they need a pep talk. I felt so isolated and so alone because I don't really talk to anybody else, just through the email loop and that's been a big help.

Rachel

We have a mentor program where at first it was nice. They would feed us dinner after school and we would have these cheesy little group activities and we had a mentor who's supposed to come in and observe our class every once in a while, check-up on us, make sure everything's fine. My mentor came in here once for maybe ten minutes so that I could sign a paper saying that I'd done it and all the other times I just signed the paper saying that she had done it, that she'd been in.

It would have been nice to have somebody that I could just talk to and say, "Hey, do you have any materials for To Kill a Mockingbird?" I just feel like everybody's so busy and everybody else is stressed out trying to do their own thing that it's just hard to have somebody to talk to about things and get material and ideas from.

They had these people at the beginning of the year; it was called Right Talk, or something, these seminars. I don't know if it's supposed to motivate us, but it was once a week for a month on Tuesday afternoons. We get out of school at two, the bell rings at 2:15; we can leave at 2:30. It was from 2:30 to 5:30 every Tuesday. And we're supposed to be excited about it? I'm sure they paid a gagillion dollars for these people. The last thing that we want to do is get out of class and then go sit in the library and listen to people talk. I couldn't even tell you what it was about and everybody's just sitting there looking mad and disgruntled because they have to be there.

Jennifer

We are assigned an in school" buddy" to help us learn their policies and operations. I also have a mentor who takes up my planning time twice a week. I'm really starting to get impatient with her. Nice lady and all, but I swear she thinks I'm an idiot—which does get under my skin after a while. But, I guess I'll jump through whatever hoops are thrown at me! [The] assigned mentor, a retired teacher, has to make contact once a week. They conduct informal and formal observations, help plan lessons, help grade papers, point out that their material is much better for use than yours, and otherwise get in your way and waste your time. She brought lesson plans and materials for the units being studied,

observed classes, and discussed my progress with the principal. She was quite
pesky at first, but we got things ironed out somewhere along the way. She began
with a very condescending attitude that rather irritated me.

CASE #4: MAKING IT ON THEIR OWN

The situations in this case reveal one important aspect of the mentoring and induction relationship: the new teacher's inability to articulate his or her needs. While Shawn and Kathleen felt confident in their ability to teach, when they thought they might need assistance, neither had the confidence to ask. While mentors and administrators cannot be mind readers, they should never expect new teachers to know everything about teaching, the school, or its unwritten rules and expectations. It is ultimately the responsibility of the administration to be proactive and ask their new teachers how they are doing and what, if anything, they could do to help them make the transition from the university to the school or from one school to another.

Shawn's case resonates with many of us who have been inducted into the profession in years past. Teachers like Shawn are often sent into classrooms with little or no support. Shawn has the benefit of being placed in a school where his colleagues are willing to assist upon request. This is a benefit and should be the professional obligation for all educators, but what happens if Shawn does not reach out? If he does not reach out or does not know whom to reach out to, Shawn could end up teaching and learning in isolation. Schools cannot assume that new teachers will ask for help; in fact, many new teachers are reluctant to do so out of a fear of appearing to be weak or ill-prepared. Both teachers in these cases appear strong enough and willing to ask for assistance as needed, but they both recognize that there is no formal support network. While Shawn appears to enter the profession as a strong candidate as evidenced by his electronic portfolio, school leaders must not assume that he is ready to be independent or not need any induction or support.

Nicole and Erin's cases brings up a different perspective that is often lost in teacher support discussions. They both enter the school year late, and Erin does so in an interim capacity. School administrators are not usually planning for this situation in that it is their goal to have vacant positions filled with full-time teachers during the summer; however, this is not always the case. Even though Erin is an interim teacher, she still requires that same support system as any other new teacher. Disregarding interim teachers may increase the lack of stability and inconsistency from the school culture. While school leaders may not want to invest resources and time into part-time teachers, not doing so may have negative consequences for students as well as the teachers.

Shawn

As far as orientation goes, nothing helpful. No mentor –here is your room, your key, good luck! Luckily I have great co-workers and went through a great education program. When I got here I was kind of on my own. My digital portfolio kind of screwed me. They're like, "Wow, this is amazing. You're fine," and just left me there and I was like, "Oh, okay."

They're all, especially the department head and the AP English teacher across the hall, so nice and helpful. There was no official mentoring, but I had good people that I work with and on their own, they're like, "If you need anything, come ask." So they're very helpful when I had questions. Then, actually one of the other coaches was like, "let me show you some of these paperwork tricks." So, there's nothing official. It's just there happened to be some really good people here that came to help out. So, I think some teachers are just out of luck; if they don't work with good people, I don't know what they do.

Kathleen

I think that a lot of schools already do some [mentoring], I just haven't necessarily got [it] around here, even principals stopping in once in a while and checking in on you. I have a unique situation having been here last year as an intern and I already have built in mentors, basically. I know I can go to any of my colleagues and ask them for help or ideas or resources on anything. I feel comfortable doing that; if I was at any other school I'm not the type that would probably go out and do that. I would be forcing myself to find all of the resources on my own and that would be really difficult, just because that's my personality. There wasn't any kind of formal situations set up to help anybody new and I think they could work on that.

Nicole

Being dropped into three classes of freshmen two weeks after school has started has NOT been anything but a nightmare. First of all, I have no classroom and no cart. I have nowhere to put my things, and I have already "misplaced" a few school supplies. The kids have had no structure, no discipline, and no instruction for 10 days. They are like wild animals. They walk around in the middle of class, talk when I am talking, threaten each other, and cuss like sailors. I am actually afraid of at least three of them. And there are almost 40 of them in each of my classes. . . . They are STILL supposedly working on schedules (even though this will be the third week of school).

I seriously don't know what to do or where to start. I don't have a clue what I am doing, and nobody seems to be able to help me out. As far as I can tell, they don't even know I'm there. My name isn't on any of the mail or things that end up in "my" mailbox (which is also mislabeled). I have no way to access my email or even use the copy machine in the library, because they haven't given me an access code yet. The kids don't have enough desks, and there aren't enough textbooks for them. They actually had to share them to read a story, and we aren't supposed to let anyone take one home. How in the hell am I supposed to teach them anything? I can't even figure out what I am doing.

My mentoring happened on its own, actually. A woman in the Spanish department somehow adopted my lost little soul one day, and I couldn't have made it without her. She talked to me after school on a regular basis. I cried, yelled, cussed and sometimes just asked her questions. She was wonderful. The school did pair me up with a "formal" mentor (my department head). She did not attend one meeting or contact me outside of school once. Some of the "mentors" were reluctant to become truly involved. Are they not setting some of us up for failure?

Erin

New teachers who were hired into permanent positions in the county were supposedly assigned mentors, although many of them say that they have not had much contact with these mentors, and that they are not necessarily someone from the same department. There was a new teacher luncheon last week where we filled out surveys, ate lasagna, and I won some flowers. Those of us who started out in interim or supply positions were basically just thrown in there without guidance, other than a meeting downtown where we learned about our insurance options and protecting ourselves from blood borne pathogens. So, much like the internship year, the new teachers have been each other's own best support system.

Lisa and Mike's Analysis

While we commend school districts for attempting to do something for new teachers, such as creating an online support network, we are troubled at how it was set up and what was required of the novice teachers. Just because technology is there, and just because someone wants a support group, does not mean it will happen. As Dan said himself, "The fact that . . . I have to go to a website set up by the county and report to a discussion board much like this one only far less rewarding or comforting because I'm conversing with teachers I've never met before and have no bond with is absurd." In other words, creating and maintaining a successful support group takes time and desire. Teachers who participate in such groups should know each other well and have a sense of responsibility and caring towards each other. Grouping total strangers and asking—or forcing—them to divulge their teaching fears and weaknesses in a public forum is not conducive to creating meaningful dialogue. The teacher education program support group worked so well for participants because members had known each other for at least two years and they were willing, voluntary participants.

Another issue for us concerns how much time was spent on two concurrent induction programs that took valuable time away from planning, teaching, and grading. Kasey and Dan, for example, were frustrated that they had to drive across town—30 minutes or so—to participate in more induction activities. The information learned in these meetings, moreover, could have been shared over email or phone. Again, novice teachers or teachers new to a district frequently need this time more for planning for their teaching than completing paperwork or activities. While induction programs should be in place, they should also be flexible enough so that those who do not need certain scaffolds (such as learning technology) can be exempted from participating.

Schools and systems have become keenly aware of the need to provide support systems for new teachers. Unfortunately when a systemic approach is applied using the same concepts of bureaucracy and paperwork, the result of a good idea can look like the situation that the novices experienced. Kasey identifies this by quoting one of the induction leaders who says, "You know, well if you leave the county we don't want you to leave because you said you didn't have enough help or you didn't have enough support."

This statement comes from the direction of school leaders to support new teachers in a verbal "attempt" to retain them. If novices do in fact leave the school or system, it is not because of a lack of support. Too often, the support comes in the form of documentation instead of strong support from mentors and other colleagues. Schools and systems can then say that they have "supported" this new teacher as evidenced by the checklist, portfolio, and other documented methods instead of actually identifying the needs of the individual new teacher. While it is not feasible to provide an individualized induction plan on each new teacher, there may be some need for choice or options based on experience and identified needs.

Questions for School Administrators

Do you have a formal mentoring program? If so, consider the following questions:

* Who leads your school or system mentoring program?
* Who assigns mentors?
* Is there a process in place to identify and match mentors with new teachers?

- Are the requirements of your mentoring program beneficial to a new teacher or do they serve as extra work and documentation?
- How do you assess the impact of your mentoring program from the perspective of new teachers?
- Are new teachers surveyed periodically so as to make individual and program adjustments?
- How are mentors evaluated?
- How much of the mentoring and induction program in your school is dedicated to the needs of your new teachers?
- How are the needs of your new teachers assessed prior to mentor assignment and the development of the year's induction program?
- New teachers need support in developing the craft of their teaching, how is this done in your school or system's program?
- Do new teachers have options in their induction based upon their individual strengths and weaknesses or are all new teachers held to the same program?
- How do you evaluate your mentoring program?
- When a new teacher enters your school or system, who is the first peer that makes contact with them?
- Who is the first person who explains the school culture to them?
- Who has the responsibility of assisting a new teacher apply local and state standards and objectives to their particular teaching assignment (s)?
- Is there money set aside for mentor training?
- Do you have support systems for interim or temporary teachers?

If you don't have a mentoring program, what barriers prevent its creation and implementation? Do you ask new teachers for feedback regarding their first year in your school or system?

ADDRESSING THE ISSUE

The suggestions and questions that follow can assist in examining what is in place, if you have a mentoring program, and offering starting points for creating a program if your school or system does not have one. Likewise, as with nearly everything else, the Internet offers a multitude of information regarding effective programs already in existence and professional development options for schools and systems looking to create programs.

Administrators need to be convinced that the mentoring process can help all stakeholders in the school; they need to consider their mentoring skills and educate themselves in areas that they are weak; they need to carefully create and train mentoring teams in order for them to "sell" the idea to staff; they should participate and mentor teachers themselves and; they should encourage recently mentored teachers to become mentors (Fibkins, 2002). At the school level, mentoring teams need to gauge their school's willingness to welcome change and new initiatives. Fibkins (2002) also recommends considering the following questions:

a. Is there a climate of collegiality? Collaboration?
b. Are staff members willing to experiment and take risks with new approaches?
c. How have prior supervisory experiences been perceived by teachers?
d. How have past staff development efforts been implemented and received?
e. What are the school's core values? What do faculty and staff deem important?
f. Does the leadership team support mentoring?
g. What other issues and/or initiatives does the school face?
h. Will the "bureaucratic structure" support mentoring?
i. How do decisions that affect the whole school get made? Top down or shared ownership?
j. What is the culture of the school? How open and flexible is the school?

There are several options for professional development in the areas of induction and/or mentoring. Professional organizations are a good first step in locating the many different professional development opportunities. The National Education Association (NEA) website, for example, provides some excellent tools to aid in planning and implementing an induction and/or mentoring program. In addition, the NEA Foundation offers web-based resources documents on creating a mentoring program, based on proceedings from the NFIE's Teacher Mentoring Symposium, co-hosted with United Teachers Los Angeles in February 1999. Topics include "The Usefulness of Mentoring" and "Selecting, Training, and Supporting Mentors." See http://www.neafoundation .org/publications/mentoring.htm.

If you are looking for a series of reports and/or websites related to specific mentoring issues, then the Education Development Center's (EDC) Center for Science Education is wonderful source of information. Topics are arranged by question, such as "How can videotapes be used to support mentors and mentees," with appropriate links to information that specifically addresses them. Some links will lead you to articles, while others will lead to products and services to assist you. The Center for Teaching Quality, based in North

Carolina, also offers a tremendous amount of information and resources for improving teaching and promoting teacher leadership (http://www.teaching quality.org/).

If hands-on training is what you are looking for, then there is the New Teacher Center at Santa Cruz (newteachercenter.org).The New Teacher Center offers comprehensive workshops on teacher mentoring ranging from "Foundations in Mentoring" to "The Site Administrator's Role in Supporting Beginning Teachers."

Chapter Two

Help with Discipline

Classroom management consistently ranks as one of the top concerns of our pre-service and novice teachers. Many often lament that they do not have such a course during their teacher preparation programs; however, can one course really prepare beginning teachers for the multiple classroom management and discipline issues they will face?

Beyond the standard techniques we often teach, such as modeling appropriate behavior and implementing consistent classroom procedures, oftentimes the discipline procedures that work in classrooms stand in opposition to what students read in their education textbooks. We both remember many things that were supposed to work with our students but didn't. Likewise, we tried things that should not have worked, but did.

Pre-service teachers are often in difficult positions during their field experiences and student teaching placements. For example, students are sometimes placed with teachers who are very lax when it comes to classroom management. One that we know of lets students bring in and eat fast food during classes—something totally against school rules. Another lets students wander in and out of the room, openly disrespect her, and yell across the room, behaviors most teachers would not allow. Still, there are others who are so strict that the classroom becomes just as negative a learning space.

While students can read about classroom management and appropriate discipline, until they actually practice it, it is often just theory. And, if they are not given the opportunity to practice it during their teacher education programs, it will take them a long time to learn and master it on the job—if they even ever get to that point. How can teacher education programs better prepare pre-service teachers for the multitude of classroom behavior issues they will face? How can teacher educators prepare them to have conversations with administrators regarding student discipline?

Case #5 focuses on Jennifer and the tough time she had with one particular class during her first year of teaching. Using emails written from August 2004 to January 2005, we show how the situation progressed and how Jennifer dealt with it. It would be simple to assume that Jennifer's classroom management and discipline problems were her own fault, either because she was too nice or didn't enforce rules. However, having observed Jennifer during her internship, I (Lisa) can attest that she was very good at classroom management. She never treated students as her friends, nor did she have any problem exerting her authority.

So, when she began posting emails to the listserv, I was concerned. Statements like, "I am finally getting some satisfaction from the administration. It appears they deal with things swiftly and strictly after I have gone through 6 previous levels of punishment" indicated that discipline was a school-wide problem, not something indicative of her room. To have to go through six levels of punishment before a student can face more serious consequences only empowers students while, at the same time, removing power from teachers (and administrators). Students are very savvy, and they readily know when a school is under their control. Many who teach in schools like this frequently give up even trying to discipline students, let alone worry about classroom management. This leads to even more problems for faculty and staff.

Troubling for us was Jennifer's comment a few days later: "I'm finally getting some attention from the office, and they are now willing to accept that I have 'exhausted my resources.'" So what resources must a novice teacher exhaust before getting the help he or she needs? How bad did the classroom situation have to become before Jennifer (or any other teacher) could count on her administrators to assist her? Jennifer should not have had to wait that long before getting help. Worse than how the students' actions affected her is how their problems detracted from instructional time. Classmates of "problem" students are often afraid to speak up for their right to an education in fear that they—instead of or in addition to the teacher—might be the next target.

Most disconcerting, however, is Jennifer's quote about her principal: "The principal, who was helping me at the beginning of the year got sick and has been gone all year, returned yesterday. He was surprised to still see me alive and well because he figured one of the 2nd period students would have jumped me by now." For an administrator to know the extent of the problems and take them lightly, is unconscionable. Moreover, to make light of them is just bad taste. Is this really the message that administrators want to send to new faculty? To all faculty? Is "jumping a teacher" something that administrators expect to happen? If so, then they are doing a poor job of running their school.

Jennifer is much stronger than most novice teachers. Reading her postings from an administrator's perspective, my (Mike) first observation is how unwilling she is to allow the realities of teaching deter her from her goals.

Regardless of how strong Jennifer is coming into this profession, her scenario represents the majority of new teachers in their first years of teaching. School leaders are sometimes quick to place blame on preparatory programs; conversely, preparation programs are quick to place blame on school leaders. Preparing new teachers, especially in the area of classroom management, is the responsibility of both.

One argument I often hear in this area is that the teachers should be better prepared to provide engaging activities, therefore reducing classroom management issues. As a result, new teachers come in with cooperative learning activities and hands-on, inquiry-based activities, all of are necessary for genuine learning. The challenge to these strategies and methods of teaching and learning is that new teachers are ill-equipped for the context in which they will implement the strategies. Such is the case with Jennifer.

CASE #5: JENNIFER

August 2004

My second period can honestly be described as Hell Raisers. They are emotionally disturbed, but since only 6 of them have learning disabilities, it is not considered an inclusion class. I'm sure they are going to be the death of me! I hope to wrangle them into submission—at least somewhat—very soon. Any ideas about dealing with tried and true "gangsta's" and "wangsta's"? I'm trying to help them not say they are all idiots. They are all self proclaimed dummies and don't think they have it in them.

August 2004

My Dept. Head from last year has dubbed my 2nd period students as the "Little Shits" (I emailed him and other previous mentors for help). I have finally dealt the killing blow in that class! I have finally exhausted my resources! The next time any problem child gets on my nerves—anything—he will be placed the "Alternative Learning Community" trailer—very hard core learning! I am finally getting some satisfaction from the administration. It appears they deal with things swiftly and strictly after I have gone through 6 previous levels of punishment. I say that by the end of next week I will have all good classes.

September 2004

My class finally hit rock bottom on Wednesday . . . Two boys started fighting in the classroom as the tardy bell was ringing. I was afraid that one of them would die in the fight—seriously, I'm talking death! The office and help is three to five minutes away, and the only other teachers in the building are older women with osteoporosis. So, that left me to break it up. I prepare myself for a broken nose and jump in the frenzy. I was victorious in separating the two without receiving so much as a scratch. Another teacher watched the class while I escorted the two to the office. I had to stay in the principal's office with the two. Meanwhile, back in my classroom, a male student attacked a female student and proceeded to beat her with her high heel shoe. It was picture day, so her yearbook picture will be bloody. Also, one student that failed to show up to class was actually in a fight behind one of the buildings—so she was in trouble. By Friday, I had 8 of 30 students on 10 day suspension for one thing or another. I'm finally getting some attention from the office, and they are now willing to accept that I have "exhausted my resources."

October 2004

I have had one helluva second period—20 out of 24 of which have spent at least one night in jail. They are violent and combative. I was terrified all year, so they pretty much ran the class. I finally got tired of it one day and quietly snapped. I lectured them how this wasn't East W—(bad side of town where they all live), we do not have to assert dominance by violence, we will not fly our gang colors proudly, we would not use random objects for weapons (staplers, yard sticks, etc) and we will not use each other's street/gang names (pistol, projects, five fingers, mad dog, etc.). I explained that we were all equal and on one playing field and that aggression was no longer welcome.
To get to the point . . .
We have been reading the Illiad and the Aeneid in class. After we read book 22 of the Aeneid, they were extremely upset that we weren't going to finish it. They protested and agreed to a more difficult test/project if I let them read it. These kids loved the Aeneid—something I thought completely impossible. They also had some very interesting real life connections (apparently Aeneas is a lot like one of the gang leaders). These students have been responding to most everything in a positive attitude. Pistol, a once very aggressive, combative, and uninterested student, now goes by Ron and brings a pencil to class. Another student, War, got shot doing something stupid and actually requested make-up work to do while he was healing.
The principal, who was helping me at the beginning of the year got sick and has been gone all year, returned yesterday. He was surprised to still see me alive and well because he figured one of the students would have jumped me by now.

November 2004

My frustration is the complete and total lack of student responsibility for their actions. I'm sick and tired of this keep them in school because of NCLB—even if they set a kid on fire! Yeah that kid is still in my class—lighter and all. The principals

*are like, "Look, I know you want us to kick them out, and they should be kicked
out, but it doesn't look good if we kick them out—so deal with it." My new motto
at school is "Ask forgiveness, not permission" with the administration.*

January 2005

*It has been a constant struggle of who actually was in charge, them or me. It
has gone back and forth. Recently though, things have changed, I am always in
charge. Last week a few tried to pull the we are stronger than you behavior, and
I snapped. In my tirade, I referred to them as little shits—my principal assured
me that teachers are allowed to snap like this once a semester. Anyway, one kid
raised his hand and without sarcasm asked, "If we are the little shits, can we
call you the Big Shit—as you actually are the one in charge."*

LISA AND MIKE'S ANALYSIS

Jennifer clearly knows her subject and has a grasp on the classroom. Administrators who read her posts will applaud the expedited time in which she seems to gain confidence, skill, and tact in dealing with her challenging students. The problem in this case is that this scenario represents many first year teachers' cases and not all new teachers have the vigor that Jennifer appears to exhibit. One of the first realities that administrators and teacher preparation programs can deal with is the overwhelming negative feelings that new teachers encounter when their students do not respond to their efforts.

Jennifer has had professionals with experience and leadership essentially tell her that her students are not good. While she may have experiences that support some of these descriptors, the leadership should have used their knowledge of the students to prepare her for the classroom instead of resorting to pre-labeling a group of students. It seems that the "sink or swim" approach was implemented, but Jennifer refused to sink. While some may argue that there is learning in this approach, it is also how we lose teachers and it is not how any other profession inducts new members. Imagine how different Jennifer's experience might have been and how much more of an impact she might have had on her students if she was prepared for the context of her school and classes.

Administrators prepare new teachers for situations this in different ways. One such way is by orienting them to the realties of their classrooms early in their induction process, ideally before hiring and immediately upon hire. Being honest and open about these challenges allows the new teacher to understand the challenges in advance and accept responsibility for them.

If the teacher is not willing to accept the challenges prior to being hired, then it is best for the teacher and the students. Once the teacher accepts the position, then it becomes necessary to acquaint him/her with the realties of the classes to the extent possible. This can be done by observing summer school classes, having open and honest dialogue with peers, working with a mentor, and other such ways. It is important, though, that the new teacher accept these as challenges and not promote negative stereotypes of students.

Another observation from Jennifer's case is her own interpretations of her students. Because she does not have anybody to help her process her observations in a positive manner, Jennifer's unenthusiastic remarks about her students become affirmed by her supervisors and colleagues. This type of induction allows for the challenges of teaching to be turned into disadvantages and negatives. What would have been more helpful in this case is if Jennifer had someone with whom she could discuss her observations so that she could learn from them and how to react to them more productively. An example is when she refers to her students as being lazy. While her students may not possess the same aptitude and work ethic that she is accustomed to or that she assumed her students would possess, this creates an ideal learning opportunity for the new teacher. With the assistance of leadership and collegial support, she may identify how the issue of laziness is a manifestation of other issues within each student and come to understand "where the students are coming from."

The next issue in this case is the one that Jennifer keenly articulates is related to administrative support. Her reference to exhausting her resources is one that resonates in schools for administrators and new teachers. This is a difficult position for administrators because one teacher's perception of exhausting resources and another's are often not the same. Jennifer could have used administrative support earlier in her experience, but it appears that she was left alone because she was mostly handling it. Administrators should never mistake a new teacher's efforts or ability to handle a classroom as competence and experience. In an effort to make sure that the teacher is responsible for his/her own classroom, administrators mistakenly guide teachers by telling them to exhaust their own resources before calling for help from an administrator. This guidance, without proper clarification, can be misinterpreted by teachers, especially those new to a school. To a new teacher, this guidance can be translated as, "Handle your classroom and don't rely on me or you don't need to work here." Regardless of the skill and strength of new teachers, it must be assumed by administrators that each new teacher requires support, assistance, and professional development in the area of classroom management.

Questions for Administrators

While this case lends support for tiered certification and enhanced clinical time for pre-service teachers so that they can gain more hands-on experience in the classroom, it is still necessary for administrators to provide support, guidance, and professional development for new teachers in the area of classroom management.

In an effort to do so:

• How can administrators prepare their new teachers for the realities of the classroom in a relatively short period of time?
• What strategies might administrators utilize to allow new teachers to understand the challenges of classroom management prior to and while experiencing problems?
• How can administrators convey the challenges of the school or classroom prior to hiring without scaring the candidate away?

In Jennifer's case, we see how colleagues and supervisors alike affirmed the negatives of the students in Jennifer's class.

• How can school leaders create a climate that takes these challenges and interprets them as opportunities?
• What kind of support mechanisms must be in place to do this? Assuming that all new teachers need support and guidance in classroom management, how can schools create plans that are individualized based on the teacher's needs?

Jennifer clearly evolves through the new teacher cycle rather quickly to the point where she gains some confidence and pleasure in teaching. It is important for new teachers to know how normal some of their frustrations, problems, and inadequacies are.

• What can administrators do during this process to allow new teachers to understand the cycle?

Suggestions and Resources

Classroom management can be one of the hardest and last areas of teaching to master for both novice and experienced teachers alike. In our own work with new teachers we hear some of them say, "My professors told me not to smile until Christmas." It is hard to believe that some teacher educators are still (not only) using this outdated and flawed expression but teaching pre-service teachers that *this* is the way to classroom management. Once teachers leave colleges of education, it is the school or school system's responsibility to help them move from "novice" to "expert." Principals need to be aware of what is going on in new teachers' classrooms and be prepared to step in and assist them, even if it is only to refer them to resources.

Oftentimes, pre-service and novice teachers confuse the term classroom management with discipline. Discipline problems often occur because of poor classroom management—which is due to lack of procedures, inconsistent procedures, unclear assignment directions and/or purposes for activities. Part of being a better teacher and classroom manager is knowing why students misbehave. One unique and interesting website (http://www.discipline help.com) we came across was "You Can Handle Them All," which lists 117 different types of school misbehaviors.

Harry and Rosemary Wong have a popular series of instructional videos and texts (such as *The First Days of School*) that provide teachers with solid ideas on how to get their classrooms running smoothly. Although much of their material (e.g., the level of their language, ways of talking to students) are more likely to appeal to elementary teachers, the practices they espouse should work at all grade levels (http://www.harrywong.com). There is also a website with their free newsletters and "real" examples of the ideas in practice from K-12 classroom teachers (http://teachers.net/gazette/wong.html). They now offer online classroom management courses (see http://www.class roommanagement.com/).

Beyond books and videos, there are also professional development courses such as Discipline With Dignity, which was founded by Dr. Richard Curwin and Dr. Allen Mendler. As they note on their website, "Discipline with Dignity is a flexible program for effective school and classroom management that teaches responsible thinking, cooperation, mutual respect, and shared decision-making." I (Lisa) actually attended one of the seminars early in my teaching career and it helped a great deal. Their website has information on their seminars, books, videos, and other resources (http://www.discipline associates.com). Of course, not every method will work with every class, or even every student. But the more resources available to and provided for teachers, the better prepared they will be.

CASE STUDIES AS LEARNING TOOLS

As you can tell from the focus of this book, we find case studies to be an effective way for new teachers to learn about handling classroom management

issues. Case studies center around a problem and include a story or information about the setting (people involved, classroom context, etc.), and questions to discuss. In the field of English education, *In Case You Teach English*
(2001) by Larry Johannessen and Thomas McCann, for example, is a text
used in teacher preparation programs to foster discussion around issues that
might come up in the classroom. The authors also provide concrete directions
for writing case studies.

Based on these cases, and experiences in their field placements, I (Lisa)
have students create their own cases, adding discussion questions for their
peers to answer. We use these in class to work through issues that the pre-
service teachers face. Below are two examples of cases written by former
students. The first case was written in the spring of 2006 by a student in
my junior-level Introduction to Education course based off her initial field
placement. The second case was co-authored by seniors in my language arts
methods course during the fall 2007 semester. While case studies are used
frequently in teacher education programs, our experience is that they are not
utilized in many induction programs. We both feel that pulling real-life examples as cases can greatly assist new teachers (and administrators).

CRYSTAL: CSE FINAL EXAM CASE STUDY

Substitute Stresses

The students' usual teacher had been out all week for jury duty. Mrs. Smith
had been their teacher all week; but she had never worked with the classes
before. Mrs. Smith made several generalizations about the class levels. The
second block 11th grade English class was the "bad" kids. They were loud,
rude, and disrespectful, according to the substitute. The third period AP English class was much better; these were the "good" kids. When an AP student
became disruptive, she would tell them, "Ya'll are acting like second period.
You're supposed to be the good kids." The AP class was allowed to talk at a
normal volume through most of the class periods. Second block was yelled at
and ridiculed if there was a constant mumble.

By Friday it was very evident that the students were more than ready to
have their usual teacher back. Tensions were strong against the substitute.
While waiting on the students to enter the classroom for third period AP English, Mrs. Smith stood in the hallway beside the door. One male student from
this AP class was wearing a hat in the hallway. She met him as he walked
by and took his hat off of his head, since hats are against the rules. As she
walked back into the classroom, she put the hat on her head. The student was
very upset by that. He followed her into the classroom and made asking for

his hat back and made snide comments about Mrs. Smith wearing the hat. In reaction, the substitute snapped back. The two broke out into a very heated argument that had both of them yelling. Mrs. Smith quickly kicked the student out of class sending him to the office.

1. Was it appropriate for Mrs. Smith to make judgments on the classes based on the level of the class? Was she right in comparing the AP class to the "bad" class? Did her biases against the classes affect her classroom management?
2. What made the students dislike Mrs. Smith? Did she treat both class periods with respect?
3. What caused the hat incident to escalate so high? Was the teacher out of line by taking the hat? Could she have handled that rule infraction differently? Was she on a power trip or just following the rules?
4. Who overreacted, the student or the substitute? Who was in the right? Should the student have been sent to the office?
5. What are some ways substitutes can handle discipline problems? What does this incident say about picking and choosing one's battles? How does that apply to teachers?

GOT TO GET SOME RESPECT AROUND HERE: DEALING WITH OVERLY-ASSERTIVE, AGGRESSIVE STUDENTS BY JAYME K. BARKDOLL & AMBER CUNNINGHAM

Preview

Regardless the content area, all classroom teachers are going to be faced with one important issue – classroom management. While most of us dreamed of and hoped for that idealized schoolhouse classroom, the reality is that most teachers do not enter into such a utopian learning environment. Instead, many of us will find ourselves in schools that challenge teachers to deal with a variety of educational detractors, ranging from verbal altercations caused by racial incongruities to physical altercations caused by widespread bullying. In the following case, you will read about a teacher that struggles with a student who feels that, due to her gender, race, and physical stature, she must become overly assertive in order to gain the peer respect she so desperately seeks. Despite having addressed the problem in a lesson regarding anger management, the teacher continues to witness the same aggressive overcompensation from this student. To make matters more difficult, the student *is* the physically smallest in her grade and one of only three Caucasian students and only seven females in this particular class of twenty-five. What additional measures could this teacher take in order to alleviate some of the classroom disruptions that are caused by this student? Furthermore, how can this teacher make her overcompensating student feel as if she does not have to be in a perpetual state of defense?

Focus Questions

As you read the following case, prepare to discuss these questions: (1) What issues inside this classroom (and this school) might have triggered the student's distracting behavior? Who is responsible for making sure that these issues do not arise? (2) What would be the most efficient means of addressing and improving this student's attitude and behavior? Where and with whom should the improvement process begin?

THE CASE: Got to Get Some Respect Around Here: Dealing with Overly-Assertive, Aggressive Students

Mrs. Mason was ready to throw her hands into the air, give up, and just call it quits for the semester. Entering her fourth year, she had never experienced a class quite like this one. Frequent fighting plagued her class periods, and a general disrespect for faculty and fellow students ran rampant amongst the teenagers filling her desks. Although she had had behavior issues with nearly every student in this group, there was one particular student that stood out above the rest in terms of aggression and impudence. Never one to afflict her wrath upon faculty, the disobedient Joanna did, however, frequently disrupt class by targeting her classmates. In fact, Joanna's disruptive actions had become daily occurrences in Mrs. Mason's ninth grade English Language Arts class.

One day during the first week, just as class was about to begin, Joanna, an extremely tiny, middle-class, Caucasian female, became overly aggressive with David, a much larger, African-American student in the class. The altercation began when David accidentally brushed Joanna on the way to his seat, which in turn served as a catalyst for one of Joanna's trademark rants.

"You need to get off me," Joanna shrieked before David could even get into his seat.

"I didn't even touch you, so you need to shut up with that," David answered.

Standing to get out of her desk, Joanna yelled, "Don't tell me to shut up, cause I'll get my mom up here on you." And with that, Joanna began to move towards David, in a fashion that could only suggest that she was ready for an actual physical altercation, not just verbal.

"You need to sit back down, cause I don't want to have fight you," David hollered while still staying seated in his desk. The closer she approached, many fellow students in the class came over to David's desk in an effort to keep him from getting angry enough to actually throw a punch.

"Go ahead, fight me! I f----- dare you! I wish you would, cause if you lay one f----- hand on me, I'll turn you in for harassment so d--- fast," Joanna goaded, now breathing down David's neck and standing right in front of him.

Just before the altercation became physical in nature, Mrs. Mason stepped back into the room, away from her post right outside of her class. When the students informed her of the argument, Mrs. Mason sent both students to the counselor—a tactic that Mrs. Mason often implements, because it allows the students to be removed from the classroom and to have enough time to calm down.

Thinking that the altercation might be a one-time event, Mrs. Mason felt as if she had done a decent job handling the issue. However, her notion was to be proven wrong the very next week, as Joanna provoked another African-American male, Jamar, into a similar dispute. While the entire class was quietly taking a test, Jamar began to nervously tap his pencil against the side of his desk. Sensing the opportunity to assert her opinion, Joanna loudly announced to the class, "Whoever is tapping their pencil needs to quit, cause *some of us* are actually trying to take the test." Jamar, hearing the condescending tone in her voice, asked Mrs. Mason to "tell Joanna to quit telling everyone what to do." He went right to the teacher, just as these students had been instructed to do.

"Joanna, please remember that if there is an issue in this classroom, it is *my* job to address, not yours," Mrs. Mason politely stated.

"Oh, well, I'm just sayin' that some of us can't concentrate when he is over there doing that," Joanna retorted, refusing to let the situation fade away.

"Shut up! Didn't you hear Mrs. Mason?!" Jamar angrily responded.

"Naw, don't tell me to shut up, I'll have my mom up here so quick, and she makes more money than your whole family will *EVER* make! We'll get us a lawyer . . . "

"Joanna! There is no need for that kind of talk," Mrs. Mason intervened. "Come here; let me write you a pass to the counselor's office."

After Joanna had irately stormed out of the classroom, Jamar, now completely disturbed and quite infuriated, asked, "Mrs. Mason, why didn't you write her up? If it had been anyone else in here, you know you would have!"

Perplexed by Joanna's behavior and Jamar's last comment, Mrs. Mason had to assess what might be triggering Joanna's frequent outbursts and whether she was being consistent in her disciplinary procedures. Mrs. Mason decided to have a one-on-one conference with Joanna to get her perspective on the issue. In an attempt to establish a trusting relationship where Joanna would feel comfortable communicating her problems, Mrs. Mason began by asking the student about her other classes, her interests, and her hobbies. After a brief while, Mrs. Mason decided to bring up the two altercations that Joanna had been a part of and, subsequently, began to question the student about her aggressive, overly assertive reactions during the two disputes.

"Well, I'm really sorry Mrs. Mason, but I have to act like that. Here, if I don't stand up for myself, no one else will do it for me," Joanna immediately responded.

Mrs. Mason, stopping for a moment, answered, "Well, Joanna, if anyone makes you angry, you should either ignore it or come tell me first, rather than trying to deal with it on your own."

"Well, I got to get some respect around here. No one respects me if I don't stand up for myself."

About this time, the bell rang and the conversation between the two had to be cut off; however, in just a few sentences, Joanna had given Mrs. Mason quite a bit to think about. Mrs. Mason pondered Joanna's incessant demands for respect from her peers, but more so, she wondered what "respect" actually entailed in the minds of her students. Furthermore, what could be the contributing factors that are causing Joanna's need for respect to come out in such a hostile manner? Mrs. Mason first considered the demographics of that particular class: out of a class of 25, Joanna was one of only 7 females and one of only 3 Caucasian individuals. Added to that, Joanna was the most petite student in the class—measuring less than five feet tall and weighing no more than ninety pounds. In other words, she was easily swallowed in a crowd of her fellow classmates. This demographic was also fairly indicative of the overall racial breakdown of the school—68% African-American, 30% Caucasian, 1% Hispanic, and 1% Asian. Mrs. Mason concluded it was possible that the class and school breakdowns might be playing a role in Joanna's need for respect and approval from her peers, being that she belonged to one of the minority groups in the school.

Deciding that the students must be responsible for their actions, minority or not, she decided to do a lesson on anger management which offered suggestions for dealing with issues of respect without resorting to verbal or physical altercations. The students seemed receptive to the suggestions at the time; however, the next day, Joanna had provoked yet another verbal, almost physical confrontation between herself, and this time, a Caucasian female student named Allison. It was at this moment that Mrs. Mason nearly reached her breaking point. Obviously, the anger management lesson had not been enough, nor was the one-on-one conference; however, Mrs. Mason had run out of ideas. Would stronger punishments be the answer to her problem? What about weekly visits with the school counselor? Were Mrs. Mason's reactions giving Joanna a license to act this way? Did the school demographics fuel Joanna's need for respect? If you were Mrs. Mason, what would you do?

Questions for Discussion

1) What do you feel are the central contributing factors to Joanna's overly assertive and aggressive behaviors? Why do you think that she feels as if she is not getting the proper level of respect from her peers?
2) During the one-on-one conference, Mrs. Mason only fit in a few meaningful questions. What other questions might have been beneficial in assessing Joanna's motives and feelings? How could she have better determine why Joanna acts in such a disruptive fashion when trying to gain respect?
3) How might Mrs. Mason better determine how students measure respect in her school? How might the demographics of the school play a role in this determination process? What role could Joanna's physical stature play in her peers' perception of her?
4) What preventative measures could Mrs. Mason take to keep Joanna's outbursts at a minimum? Furthermore, in the event that Joanna does act out again, what measures could Mrs. Mason take to minimize the disruption caused by the student? Lastly, what measures could she take to discourage Joanna from escalating the altercations?
5) In each of the altercations, Joanna is the provoker and aggressor. What advice would you give a student that has been targeted by Joanna? Finally, why do you feel that Joanna views provocation as a means of garnering respect, even though students do not openly disrespect her?
6) Who is ultimately responsible for improving Joanna's behavior? Should it rely on the individual student's shoulders? What role should the other students play in the process? Is it primarily the teacher's responsibility? Where does the administration fit into all of this? Lastly, how much of this can be placed on the parents'?

Related Research and Writing

1. Read a book such as Jim Larson's *Think First: Addressing Aggressive Behavior in Secondary Schools* or Johns and Carr's *Techniques for Managing Verbally and Physically Aggressive Students* that discuss ways to handle students that have aggressive dispositions and often act on their aggressive

NEW YORK INSTITUTE
OF TECHNOLOGY

tendencies. What strategies do you find to be particularly plausible in the situations you have witnessed or been a part of? Which strategies do you feel are ineffective? Do you think that your plausible strategies would be effective in all cases? Why or why not? How large a role do you feel the individual student plays in determining how you will handle aggressive behavior?

2. Read the following articles and discuss how each article's findings relate to classroom disruptions that you have witnessed and the one that has been described in this case study:

   • Ann Read Smith's "'Teacher! Make them stop!'"
   • Daniel A. McFarland's "Student Resistance: How the Formal and Informal Organization of Classrooms Facilitate Everyday Forms of Student Defiance"
   • Gay & Parry-Jones' "The Anatomy of Disruption: A Preliminary Consideration of Interaction Sequences within Disruptive Incidents"
     Which of the preceding articles do you feel highlights the most important contributing factor to persistent classroom disruption and student disrespect? Why did you choose the article that you did? Are some contributing factors more important than others, or are they all equally as significant?

Chapter Three

Choosing Parents and Students over Teachers

Nearly every teacher has, at one time or another, felt abandoned or betrayed by an administrator or disciplinary dean. For me (Lisa), it was in my second position, at a school where the administration was not consistent with discipline. For example, upset that he had to complete an assignment in a particular way, a male African American student, in front of the whole class, equated me with a slave owner verbally accusing me of treating students like slaves. My hands shaking, I wrote a referral for disrespect. Weeks later, with no action ever taken, the referral wound up "missing" and the disciplinary dean—also the student's football coach—never addressed the incident.

The two cases featured in the chapter, Numbers 6 and 7, are similar in that at both schools teachers' concerns and needs were subordinate to students' and parents' desires. Our focus on these cases is simple: No matter how "good" a school is, if faculty feel they have no power or control or respect in their classrooms, they will not be happy—and they won't stay.

CASE #6: WHO'S IN CHARGE?

Case #6 centers on two teachers (Dan and Kasey) not feeling supported by administrators, especially when it came to student discipline. Unfortunately, their case is far too common. The frustration expressed by them is not limited to new teachers alone. Veteran teachers often express the same confusion and frustration as it relates to discipline and discipline referrals. The relationship between teacher and administrator is much like a contract. Teachers are eager and willing to teach so long as they have the support of their administration to assist with those issues that detract them from their abilities to teach. This relationship, when established appropriately, allows teachers to teach in safe,

33

orderly schools where they view their classrooms as powerful spaces that focus on students and learning. Student discipline and working conditions are too often the factors contributing to good teachers leaving the profession.

The role of school administration is to serve as a resource for teachers so that teachers can focus on teaching. While teachers are often unaware of the many issues that administrators must consider when reviewing discipline referrals, there is no excuse for not communicating back to teachers. It must become the mindset of the administrator that if a teacher spent the time writing the referral then it merits a response and an action. Arguably, not all discipline referrals are valid. School administrators deal with voluminous amounts of referrals ranging from minute to major issues; however, to the teacher each one is important. These are the details that, if unattended, have major negative repercussions on a faculty's impression of the leadership and culture of the school.

School leaders and veteran teachers might erroneously assume that new teachers know what constitutes a referral and how to write one. Successful administrators have dealt with this issue in a number of ways. For new teachers, an orientation to the student code of conduct and the process for writing referrals may be helpful. Establishing clear processes for discipline referrals is also necessary. The process must be one that is supported by the school and the leadership. Some school administrators study the turn-around time on discipline referrals to ensure that they are processed in a timely manner, usually the same day.

Regardless of the action taken by the school official, the response must be communicated back to the referring teacher. For new teachers, the written communication may be followed up by conversations with the administrator related to the referral. Debriefing conversations allow the administrator to provide new teachers with the expectations regarding student discipline. Such conversations also allow new teachers to learn more about the process of referrals, what to write on them, and what to expect as far as actions. These professional conversations may also provide the novice teacher with strategies and suggestions for classroom management as provided by the administrators.

As school leaders and teachers work together toward student success, there many times seems to be a relationship of tension between both parties when it comes to student referrals. The reasons for this run the gamut. In some cases, student misbehavior could have been prevented with proper teacher intervention, teaching strategies, and professionalism. In some cases, it is difficult to articulate the severity of the classroom offense on a discipline referral, so administrators act on what is provided to them without consulting the teacher first. At times, school officials learn more about the student and the misbehavior after or during the discipline conference. Again, there are many reasons for this, but communication is essential.

Safe and disciplined schools require responsive leadership, especially in the area of student discipline. Administrative teams must honor an open door policy for all teachers. A mentality and expectation must be present that require administrators and deans to drop whatever it is they are doing when a teacher asks for help. While the day of an administrator is overwhelming, there should be nothing more important than a teacher asking for assistance. For too many teachers, this is an area that negatively impacts their decision to remain in teaching.

At the end of Kasey's first year teaching, when asked about some low points of the school year, she focused on lack of discipline and related the following story which has been transcribed from an interview with her.

I have this one student . . . I think he's got ADD, or ADHD, but he's annoying all the time. You write him up and you send him down there [to the office], but he is still annoying every single day. We had an incident last Friday where two administrators came in and there was some money stolen and nobody was going to leave until we got everybody's names down.

The kid was like, "I gotta bus to catch."

And the administrator was like, "You don't even ride a bus. I see you walking."

KID: "I ride a bus, I ride a bus, you can walk, come on, I show you I ride a bus."

ADMINISTRATOR: "You need to stop with your attitude."

KID: "Whatever."

OTHER ADMINISTRATOR: "You need to stop it or you're gonna go home and take your finals next year."

KID: "Whatever"

Then he got up when everybody was leaving. The kid got up and walked up to the administrators, walking past them.

We've written him up three times in the last two weeks. I don't know if the administrator or if the discipline people are just like, "Hey it's the summer, so I'm not gonna punish anybody anymore," but nothing has happened to him. When they were leaving I was like: "I'm so sorry about him. We've written him up three times."

ADMINISTRATOR: "Oh that's just, you know, whatever the kid's name is."

To me, that's a lot of complacency. That's probably been a low point but the other low point is the fact that you do write them up and you, but half of the time depending on which administrator gets [the referral] or what kind of mood they're in they don't do anything. I mean, this kid's been written three times; he's probably the one who stole the money and it's just like Oh, well, that's just how he is. There's no excuse for it. I don't think there's any excuse for it. I had another incident where this one girl never showed up for my class and I checked to see if she checked and she hadn't, so I wrote her up. When the referral came back it said she was down in Mr. So and So's office, who is a disciplinarian. He's not even her disciplinarian. It's alphabetized; so she just went down there and spent the whole class time talking to him. Then I look like the idiot because I wrote her up for no apparent reason. But he's a coach; he's black, and most of the black kids, the black girls go to him or talk to him.

I emailed him. It said next time one of my students is going to be down there past five minutes, I want you to email me and let me know because I didn't know where she was and I wrote her up. Then he emailed me back and he's like well it's very difficult because I'm taking care of the letters H through N and, but I'll try next time. If it's so difficult, then why did you talk to a student for an hour and a half that's not even on your list?

Dan validated Kasey's story, also offering up his own example of how his discipline referrals went ignored.

I did have one kid that I wrote up two times in the same week and, to my knowledge, nothing's been done. Even when you do write up a kid, you don't find out what happened to them. There's no reporting back and you don't have any communication unless you walk all the way down there yourself. Not to say that is shouldn't be done, but that takes a lot of time when really it should be taken care of without me having to leave my classroom or my desk.

LISA AND MIKE'S ANALYSIS

Both Kasey and Dan touched on a key issue: communication. Everyone who works in schools is busy, but time must be made for adequate and appropriate contact. To try to resolve the issue and open up the lines of communication, Kasey did send an email to the discipline dean requesting that if he needs to hold a student in his office for more than a few minutes to please let her know so she won't erroneously write a referral. And, yes, he did respond. However, the issue is that his response did not address the main concern: Why is he entertaining students not under his charge in his office for an entire class period? As a first-year teacher, Kasey has a decision to make—does she stand her ground and press the issue further, or does she let it go so as not to make matters worse? Does she have someone (a peer, a mentor) to get advice from?

Dan's situation is one that many teachers are, unfortunately, all too familiar with: discipline referrals that never get addressed. As teachers, we have had this happen. Almost nothing is more frustrating than to have student misbehavior unpunished. If it happens once a year, or because of extenuating circumstances, that is acceptable. However, when ignoring teachers' referrals becomes a pattern, it sets the tone for how the school runs. And, students quickly learn how much they can get away with. Once that happens, the locus of power shifts, and the adults in the building are no longer in charge.

CASE #7: "FU*# TEACHING"[1]

Shawn's case is a situation of expectations and knowledge of school guidelines. An assumption is too often made that new teachers have been through a professional training program that equips them for all the roles and expectations placed on them in teaching. What these programs do not do and in many ways cannot do, is prepare teachers for the context and the culture of individual schools. New teachers often enter the profession without the experience and knowledge of the numerous situations in which they will be placed on a daily basis. They are placed into a profession that requires immediate and constant decision making without the safeguards of university advisors and cooperating teachers. Without proper induction and guidance, new teachers are unequipped to handle the numerous situations that they will encounter.

Procedures, processes, and expectations must be known by all faculty and staff in the school. Procedures for handling a situation like the one Shawn encountered should not be left to learning by experience. Teachers are put into positions like Shawn's often and they must know how to navigate and act without relying on impulse. How differently Shawn may have handled this situation if he were presented with the guidelines up front? Unfortunately, we will never know. Veteran teachers have experience as their guide that directs their actions. Novice teachers have little background on such situations. They are unaware of how to de-escalate a situation, how to respond procedurally when confronted with such a student, and how to handle the situation professionally. These are the procedures and guidelines that must be presented by the school leaders before allowing new teachers to enter the classroom.

Shawn's story, sadly, goes way beyond ignored referrals or complacent administrators to what can happen when teachers are made to feel (and look) completely powerless in front of students, parents, and other teachers (see Scherff, 2008 for more details). The beginning of Shawn's story is similar to that of other first-year teachers; he felt prepared to teach and was thrilled about getting a paycheck. Shawn was pleased to receive a job offer at a high school noted for being one of the top high schools in the country.

Although initially he pointed out that discipline would be strict, and that was one reason he was thankful to be working at the school, Shawn shortly found this not to be the case, at least for students. He voiced this concern many times over the course of our e-mails. Shawn also noted the power that students and parents held: "these kids know you can't do anything to them. Like if you fail a senior, there's a good chance you're gonna see lawyers . . . there's a good chance you're gonna see at least parents talking about lawyers."

While several times (like above) he had mentioned how teachers were made to feel more like the students every day, there was little foreshadowing of the events that transpired during the fall 2004 semester. We learned about it in an October email:

> *I am a little too pissed now to fully talk about it but a student I was escorting out of class turned on me and shoved me both hands in my chest—I held him down on the ground until the principals came—whose suspended—me—what am I waiting for—see what the parents and students feel—BULLSHIT! Does anybody care that I was attacked first—doesn't look like it. Does the boy have a mark on him—no. Did I do anything that is illegal in a high school athletic competition—no. Did he—yes. Fu*# teaching.*

The Fallout

Whether Shawn violated the student's rights, broke any school rules, or assaulted the student is unknown. However, what is acknowledged is that Shawn was never given the opportunity to tell his story or defend himself regarding the incident. Statements were taken from his students, but Shawn was not permitted to respond to them. In essence, Shawn was made defenseless while the students were given power—with their narratives going unchecked. He was sent home immediately, and indefinitely. His repeated calls to the school were not returned. The union eventually advised him to resign. His e-mail is below.

> *I waited three weeks for the first word. I called my principal 3 times in the first week and a half. The first two times she told me to be patient while it was being worked out. The third time I heard that the kid who pushed me never missed a day of school. When I asked her why a kid who pushed a teacher was at school and the teacher wasn't—she said that I was the only one who said he pushed me. I never called her again—she has never called me. I talked with my state union representative only—after 3 cancelled meetings by the superintendent—she fi-*

nally was able to see him last Thursday. He said that it was in my best interest to resign and would give no further information. The three other assaults that happened in the county while I have been gone have been settled with no teachers leaving. I am waiting to meet with a lawyer on Thursday, but I will just be trying to get the most paychecks out of my resignation. I don't even have the desire to fight this. Loud parents, bad kids, and politics are what education is about and this kid is bad, his parents are loud, and I am in a very political school system.

LISA AND MIKE'S ANALYSIS

Although Shawn acknowledged that conceivably he should have not touched the student at all (and learned unspoken rules: "just let the kids hit each other"), he insisted that he only protected himself. He felt that at his school outward perceptions were important, and maintaining them meant that parent and student desires took precedence over teacher professionalism and respect. His school was one where administration seemed to promote student and parent's interests over those of its staff.

While teacher education programs can try to prepare teacher candidates through coursework, case studies, and the internship itself, ultimately, school administrators must claim some responsibility for novice teachers' feelings of dissatisfaction. Beginning (and veteran) teachers enter a building with its own history, ways of interaction, methods of operating, and social and organizational culture (e.g., Craig, 1999; Kuzmic, 1994; Rex & Nelson, 2004; Weiss, 1999). As Shawn's story shows, the power seemed to rest not with classroom teachers, but with students (and their parents) who, in turn, influenced how administrators managed conflict. Did pacifying parents come at the expense of teacher control, decision-making, and professionalism?

Shawn needed an advocate in this incident. It appears that he was not matched with a mentor who could have inducted him into the tacit operations and expectations of the school. If Shawn had a professional peer from which he could have learned about the school's context he might have been better equipped to handle the circumstance. Mentors also serve as advocates and sponsors in difficult situations, such as the one described by Shawn. Mentors have an ability to protect and buffer new teachers from the political pressures of teaching until they are able to stand on their own. A mentor may have also been able to assist the school administration and the parents mediate this situation so that a teacher's career may have not been a casualty. It does not appear that Shawn was afforded professional, and possibly, legal rights that teachers should have in cases such as this. Minimally, Shawn's perspective should have been elicited from school administrators. In cases such as this, regardless of public or parental pressures, the rights of the teacher should be granted. Shawn should have been able to provide his perspective of the situation related to this student incident. A thorough, formal investigation may have revealed information that would assist the decision makers in this case.

Questions for Administrators

As most of these questions are also tied to induction, mentoring, and classroom management, we simply pose additional questions. The resources provided at the end of Chapters 1 and 2, apply to this chapter as well.

New teachers often have different perceptions of what should and should not be handled in the classroom. In general:

- How can school leaders articulate the referral process to new teachers? How can proper induction in this area assist?
- What can school administrators build in to the referral process that guarantees immediate feedback to the teachers once an action is taken?
- How should a new teacher be advised to inquire into the status of an open referral without trepidation for his/her job?
- Where and by whom should a new teacher learn to inquire about referrals that are not acted upon in accordance with the student code of conduct and/or the teacher recommendations?
- Especially in large schools, what system is in place to ensure that a timely response is in place for each referral placed for an administrator?

As it relates to your current school in particular:

- What is the turn-around time for a discipline referral?
- Do you meet weekly with your other school administrators to establish the expectation regarding discipline?
- If surveyed, how would your teachers rate you and if applicable your administrative team regarding the support provided to teachers?
- Shawn expressed his discontent for the political pressures of teaching. How do new teachers in your school learn the unspoken rules?
- How do you work to proactively prepare teachers for the situations or potential situations they may encounter in your classrooms?
- In your school orientation, do you walk new teachers through some of the scenarios they may encounter in their classrooms?
- Do you provide professional expectations to your new teachers or is it assumed that they know how to respond to various situations?

New teachers often do not yet possess the knowledge of being a parent themselves.

- How do new teachers in your school learn about the parents' perspective as it relates to their classrooms?
- Do you teach new teachers how to conduct parent conferences or is it assumed that they can lead them on their own?

NOTE

1 Portions of this section originally appeared in Scherff, L. (2008). Disavowed: The stories of two novice teachers. *Teaching and Teacher Education, 24,* 1317–1332.

Chapter Four

Professional Learning Communities

Luckily, the staff at my new school is unbelievable. We all have already bonded in such a way that I feel like I'm hanging out with you guys again. I feel like I'm home, and being with them helps me with missing you all and our support group—Lane

Out of all the novice teachers in the group, Lane perhaps had the most supportive situation—and that was not the result of any formal mentoring or induction program. Lane took a job at Inverness High School, a brand new high school in an affluent region of her home state. In its first year, serving only grades nine and ten, the small school setting, in addition to no prior norms or school culture, seemingly allowed teachers to create the kind of teaching climate they wanted. Even though there were many school-based issues that Lane had problems adjusting to, one thing she found was a positive teaching culture through professional learning communities. During her first year teaching, when specifically asked about mentoring at Inverness, Lane emailed, *"We have made an attempt at school at a mentoring program—while the fruition of this has not been formal, but rather just a natural thing. Luckily, the entire faculty kind of mentors each other since we are all young and such good friends."*

Lane had the most positive first-year experience, with her administrators initiating professional learning communities. Grouped heterogeneously, teachers met after school on early release days to share and discuss issues they were facing—math teachers could learn from history teachers and veteran teachers could learn from novices. Lane found it both helpful and empowering. Not only did it assist her and her colleagues learn how to respond to problematic situations, as Lane indicated, this practice spilled over into her own classroom. It is no surprise to hear that Lane is still teaching (albeit after a short break) and one of the most satisfied.

The professional learning community worked similarly to what Lane experienced and practiced during her teacher education program through the online discussion board. Such spaces allow teachers to work through issues—whether through just writing them down or through the dialogue provided by colleagues. Likewise, because she had this experience in her teacher education program, Lane knew many of the unwritten rules and codes of behavior for working in such groups. Comfortable sharing classroom problems in a more public forum, she used the school-based groups to their full potential. Because her experience was so unlike the other teachers', in the fall of 2007 we asked Lane to outline in Case #8 how her school enacted these professional learning communities and what they meant to her and the other teachers.

CASE #8: CREATING PROFESSIONAL LEARNING COMMUNITIES (AS TOLD BY LANE)

They are collaborative groups of teachers across the curriculum that meet once a month to discuss student work and any other issues that may come up. I am a collaborative group leader this year, and we have about nine people in the group. During the first meeting, we set social norms for our group time to make sure that everyone is on the same page, and it kind of reinforces some professionalism. Each time, one person presents a dilemma (or best practice) to share with the group. I choose a specific protocol beforehand that best suits the situation, and the group follows that protocol during our discussion. I like them because it eliminates a lot of tension and the opportunity for one person to dominate the conversation. Once we clarify the problem, the group brainstorms possible ideas and solutions to the problem while the presenter is silent and takes notes on the ideas.

This is the one thing that has been successful in our school over the past few years. It helps us get to know our colleagues from different curriculums, and surprisingly, we all benefit from some of the practices that are done in classrooms very different from our own. I have actually used the protocols to help facilitate my class discussions in my English classes. It involves the non-participants and the structure helps the discussion move along without a lot of crazy tangents. We also use the collaborative group model in our faculty meetings and departmental meetings.

Additionally, we are all grouped together at the beginning of the year not just according to content areas, but also to our personality styles. We do an activity called Four Corners during our first professional development day, and we are grouped based on what corner we are in (Action, Meaning, Caring, and Structure). This way groups aren't all action people or all caring people, etc. It was something that our principal wanted to implement before we opened the school. She mentioned them in our interviews and studied articles about them after we were hired and before our summer professional development. We all took really well to them because it was a new school, and it helped bond us together.

TEACHING AT INVERNESS: FROM THE BEGINNING

Lane's emails over the years of the project often conveyed her satisfaction with her colleagues and work environment as well. While she did have issues with some aspects of the school (like we all have had), overall, her initial years were much more positive than the others. Her first email to the group (August 2, 2004) is below.

I've met everyone at the school and it seems like it is the kind of school that would materialize if all of us started one; everyone seems so passionate about education like we all did in our classes over the past couple of years. I just feel so out of it though; these past two months feel like an eternity, and what used to feel so comfortable now seems scary again, as if I had never stepped foot in the classroom.

Lane also received tremendous support from her administrators, which helped to add to the backing from her colleagues. As such, when things went wrong, or when she was struggling with classroom management issues, parents, or her own self-doubt, she was surrounded by support. In October, struggling with stress-related health issues she wrote to the group about her administration:

My assistant principal tells me that by January I will be feeling much better about things. He had some really good things to say the other day; he told me that his first year he came very close to ditching the whole teaching thing and doing something else. But he stuck out the first year and ending up loving it, and now, seven years later, he is our assistant principal. I guess that is one good thing right now—our faculty and administration is so supportive and friendly; I feel completely comfortable hanging out in administrative offices and chatting with them, as well as venturing to other wings to visit with teachers of other disciplines.

Lane made it through the first year pretty much unscathed and continued on at the high school for another two years, making it through the novice three years. However, in the fall of 2007, she announced to the group that she was leaving teaching for an editorial position in the publishing industry. (Note: halfway through the spring of 2008, Lane revealed that teaching was her true love and she returned to the classroom, filling in for a teacher at another school; she returned to full-time teaching in the fall of 2008.)

MIKE'S ANALYSIS

If only each new teacher entering the profession articulated these thoughts within the first years of teaching. Lane's case appears to be an instance of what can be done to induct new teachers. While Lane readily admits that formal mentoring and induction mechanisms were not in place, there spirit of these processes certainly exists.

First, by being at a new school, Lane is not a new teacher thrown into a pre-existing school culture. Therefore, Lane is able to create her niche along with all the other teachers in the building doing the same thing. The administrator, in this case, made the wise decision to empower the teachers to create this new culture. This culture development allows Lane to be an active participant instead of a recipient; therefore, she has a greater stake in the school's success as well as her own success. This potentially allows Lane to see the global perspective of teaching that many do not begin to see until later in their careers. While current school leaders are not always fortunate to open a new school and create a culture from scratch, there is still plenty to glean from this case. School leaders have the ability to re-create cultures. While changing pre-existing school cultures may be difficult, the benefits of the process alone have advantages as seen from the perspective of Lane.

Next, Lane has touched on an important aspect of the mentoring and induction process. She states that the formal programs are not yet in place because the school is so new. However, the process of mentoring and induction, if done as a natural part of school's culture, can be more effective and longer lasting than any formal programs. The learning community spirit in this case is the mentoring and induction. The ability for the teachers to have time to engage in dialogue on issues facing them personally or as an organization is what mentoring and induction aim to achieve. The powerful conversations that can emerge have profound implications for adult learning and teacher development. As it relates to new teachers, this allows them to engage in conversation with teachers with differing levels of experience and caliber, learning from each of them as the novices develop their own teaching practices. This is the kind of dialogue that should exist in all schools.

Lastly, Lane's experiences with her colleagues not only supported her during these important years of development, but they also had a direct impact in the ways in which she taught in her classroom. This is possibly the strongest form of professional development that can occur in a school. We often think of mentoring and induction with the new teacher being the one who gains from such support. Lane's case is evidence of where the processes of mentoring and induction possibly have a direct impact on what transpires in the classroom, with the students being the most important beneficiaries.

Questions for Administrators

Lane's experience is one that can be difficult for school leaders to be able to create and sustain over time; however, that does not mean it cannot be done.

- How can school leaders immerse new teachers into a pre-existing culture as professionals?

In many schools, it is understood that new teachers have to prove themselves before they can be teacher leaders.

- How can new teachers assume leadership roles that allow them to grow personally while contributing to the school as a whole?
- What structures can principals put into place in their schools to encourage the critical dialogue that Lane experienced?
- Have you asked your teachers what they would like to see in the way of professional learning communities? Do they exist at your school? If so, how well do they work?
- How can new teachers be placed into support groups that do not have being a new teacher as the common factor?
- How can administrators audit their school culture to see if it is accepting of new teachers

Information on Professional Learning Communities

What is a professional learning community (PLC)? We like this definition: "Participants in a professional learning community interact around professional matters, focusing on pedagogy, content, and assessment. This is the center of daily work within a school" (Revisioning Professional Development, 2003, p.6). SEDL (formerly the Southwest Educational Development Laboratory) has an excellent primer on PLCs (http://www.sedl.org/change/issues/issues61.html), including an example of how one school created a professional learning community. From the initial webpage, there are numerous links to other sources of information on creating and sustaining professional learning communities. Professional Learning Communities can occur in any school and across all subjects. The March 2008 edition of *The CSP Connection* shows how PLCs were created at 27 schools in one region through the Monterey Bay Science Project (see http://csmp.ucop.edu).

If you want more information, the National Staff Development Council has a list of links to articles and websites that can help in researching, planning, implementing, and evaluating PLCs: http://www.nsdc.org/standards/learning communities.cfm.

Chapter Five

Supporting Your Teachers

Question: What could schools do to encourage teachers to stay in teaching?
Answer: I think a strong and supportive administration is a good place to
start. If the administration would control the environment of the school, develop
a practical discipline plan, and stand behind its teachers it would make a world
of difference in some areas.
–Nicole

What can principals can do to support their beginning teachers, thus increasing the likelihood that they will remain at their schools? Beaudoin and Taylor (2004) offer an equation for predicting job satisfaction:

Job Satisfaction=Connection + Collaboration + Appreciation +
Trusting Relationship with Principal – Disrespect

Connection, for them, is about the faculty being together and doing common activities. This leads to collaboration. At minimum, collaboration is simply sharing materials or handouts, but it can extend all the way to co-teaching, peer coaching, or even trading classes. To add to the job satisfaction equation, administrators need to also genuinely show their gratitude and appreciation to teachers and staff for the work they do. Finally, principals must be supportive of their teachers, being available for them to discuss issues and concerns. In essence, principals need to know how to communicate effectively (Beaudoin & Taylor, 2004). Brock and Grady (2001) contend that principals communicate what they consider important several ways:

• by what they pay attention to, comment on, ask about, praise, and criticize;

- through their responses and decisions during crisis situations;
- through the behavior they model;
- via the allocation of rewards; and
- by their criteria for recruiting, retaining, and releasing faculty and staff (pp. 35–36).

The definition of "support" varies according to who you ask. To some administrators, supporting teachers means providing adequate supplies and keeping the school in order. To others, it may mean backing the teachers on discipline issues and conflicts with parents. For teachers, however, support can mean something entirely different. Support, from our own experience and from working with classroom teachers, often means showing appreciation for a job well done. Support can also come in the form of an open-door policy and keeping teachers and staff "in the loop."

The two cases in this show the extent to which appreciation, or lack of it, and keeping teachers informed contributed to their desire to remain in the profession (or at least remain at their current school). Rachel's story is one of feeling abandoned by her principal, leaving her feeling underappreciated and alone. Kathleen's tale is one that concerns a serious incident that occurred at her high school. Teachers were not informed of the crisis; many of them viewed this as disrespectful to them as teachers and rendered them unable to assist students. In this chapter, we use both emails and interview excerpts to create fuller cases.

CASE #9: RACHEL

In May 2005 Rachel had pretty much decided that she was going to give teaching a break for at least a year. Working at an urban school had taken so much out of her that she didn't think she could get through a second year anywhere. However, many teachers work at urban schools and feel renewed and energized, so what impacted Rachel? According to her, it went beyond student apathy to the whole environment and culture of the school and both of those could be largely attributed to administration's actions.

The situation at Rachel's school is, sadly, not isolated. Many schools, particularly urban ones, face such a myriad of problems that teachers are sometimes the last ones to be supported. However, what Rachel's case also shows is that when teachers are left behind, the whole school suffers. Disrespect does trickle down and when teachers are disrespected by everyone around them, they will often give up and resort to behaving like those they interact with on a daily basis.

We can understand Rachel's feeling let down by her principal. Similar things happened to us when we taught. However, what this case teaches us is that as teacher educators, we must better prepare our candidates for the interview and hiring season. Interviews are like first dates; each party is on their best behavior. The teacher wants a job, and the principal wants a teacher. Both will frequently say and do what is necessary to have the deal sealed.

Rachel very keenly recognizes the need for strong, supportive leadership in her first year of teaching. Like most new teachers, Rachel seems to have selected her first teaching job based on the knowledge that she will be supported and nurtured during her first year in the profession. While Rachel seems to be willing to deal with the numerous challenges of teaching, she seems less inclined to do so in an environment that is apathetic and uncaring.

While Rachel is frustrated by the behavior of her students and the responses she gets from their parents, she is more disappointed that she does not have a leader who assists her in interpreting these issues. Effective school leaders are able to guide teachers through challenges and turn them into opportunities. In this case, it appears that the faculty are given challenges and then left to handle them on their own. Teachers have a tough job and are often forced to do it in isolation from their peers. For a new teacher like Rachel, who was accustomed to collegial interactions in her teacher preparation program, this is often a difficult and unnecessary transition. Rachel's focus on the "little things" is important. Teachers are motivated to do their jobs for reasons that are genuine and compassionate. Many teachers go into teaching because they see the good in children, they see the need to be a mentor, or they see themselves as positive role models. Unfortunately, we are not in a career that recognizes these goals with monetary incentives, nor is this what teachers are looking for at all times. Teachers are often simply asking for affirmation and recognition of their work. This need for praise or affirmation is even more so the case for new teachers. They are constantly looking for feedback, praise, and other methods of support in order to know if they are doing it right. In the absence of such feedback, they are forced to make conjectures and assumptions on their development as a teacher. The transcript below is from the May 2005 interview at Rachel's high school.

Lisa: What'd you think when you came and interviewed?

Rachel: I loved it. I loved it. She [the principal] was very nice to me; she was very motherly during the interview. I was really excited. She talked about the magnet program they have here and all these fabulous, wonderful things about the school . . . and I haven't seen much of it.

Lisa: You haven't seen much, so do you feel like you were fooled, or do you think that's a line to get people here or do you think that you have to earn a place in that?

Rachel: It's the teachers who have been here for 30 years who have the AP classes and the honors classes and magnet classes but I think, too . . . with the whole race issue, she told me it was 50–50 and it's not 50–50 at all but she flat out told me that it was. So, obviously, she knew better. I was really excited after the interview and I was excited [about] getting started.

Lisa: Did the principal kind of stay the same mothering [type]?

Rachel: No, no. I can pass her in the hallway and she won't even look at me or acknowledge me. I can say hello and she'll just keep on walking. Staff meetings are about "well you all need to start," "you're not keeping up with tardies," and "you're not doing this," and "you need to do this." It's the last thing that we need to hear at the end of the day whenever we're already having hard time.

Lisa: So do you ever hear about the successes or the good things?

Rachel: On our administrivia she sends out on Mondays she has the bottom section as kudos. She lists like five things good that people are doing, but then at the top there's a whole section of things that we need to do. We don't have duty free lunch here which technically in Georgia there's something in our union about we're supposed to have duty-free lunch. We have lunch duty every third week and we have once-a-month duty where we have to sit in the hallway on lockdown. We're basically on lockdown every day and all the time there's a random planning period is gone sitting in the hallway, going to this meeting, or this and that. But nope, she definitely changed. She's very good at what she does, but I think that she's just constantly business-minded and management rather than "let's take care of these people here."

Lisa: Meaning, the teachers, people?

Rachel: Teachers and students . . . I mean Christmas, you get a candy cane in your mailbox or something, you know. You get a Christmas card. Have a great break. Valentine's Day you get a Hershey's kiss in your mailbox or something. Nothing. We haven't had anything all year like that. This is teacher appreciation week and we did have a breakfast this week , but you know I feel unappreciated here. One of my friends who works here, she's 52 years old, and she's taught forever. She says she's never felt so unappreciated.

Lisa: What three things, or one or two three things could like schools and school districts do to encourage teachers to stay?

Rachel: Put a candy cane in their mailbox at Christmastime. Put a Hershey's kiss in their mailbox at Valentine's. It's the little things like that that make you feel appreciated and when you go all year without anything like that, it's just kind of, all right, do they even care that I'm here? I just think it's little things like breakfast every once in a while. We don't even have a break room. The teachers' lounge is turned into a classroom, so there's nowhere for . . . teachers to go.

Questions for Teachers and Teacher Educators

This case poses some complex questions that teachers—new and experienced—and teacher educators can ask of themselves and others:

* If you were Rachel, what would/could you have done to improve you own morale? The morale of those around you?
* If you were Rachel's colleague, what suggestions would you have for her? What could you do to help her?
* What could her fellow colleagues have done to improve working conditions at the school?
* How would you go about interacting with the principal if you worked at the same school?
* What questions should we train our teacher candidates to ask during the interview process?
* How can we prepare them to "find out" a school's culture and environment?
* Do we owe do teacher candidates a disservice by not dissuading them from going to high-need schools like that in their first year?
* How can we assist teacher candidates better during the job-seeking process?

Questions for Administrators

* How can principals ensure that each teacher gets genuine praise that is necessary for job satisfaction?
* How might a formalized induction program assist teachers in Rachel's position?
* If you were to assume a leadership position in Rachel's school, what steps would you take to support her in her first year teaching?

CASE #10: KATHLEEN

Kathleen went through a traumatic school incident like many schools have or will have to face in the future. These are the issues or incidents that may or may not shape a school, but leave an impact all the same. While school leaders are becoming much smarter on how to respond to issues like the one presented here, the perspective that is important in this case is the internal communication that appears to be absent. While administrators, depending on the situation at hand, have to make numerous tough decisions, communication with faculty and staff needs to be considered. In this case, the administration may have been directed by the police or supervisors to not communicate any information to teachers, staff, and/or students. If that was the case, it still would have been wise to inform the faculty that there was some sort of an "issue" but that nothing can be communicated about it, temporarily. While many of the teachers probably shared Kathleen's sentiments, remember she is a new teacher experiencing a major issue for the first time. It is important for school leaders not to lump all teachers in one category during these situations or in the wake of these circumstances. Teachers, depending on their needs and their career level, may need varying levels of assistance and support with situations such as the one Kathleen experienced.

The incident that occurred at her high school remained with Kathleen for a long time and, to some extent, it lessened the trust she had in her administrators. In her eyes, if there is a hint of violence, teachers should know about it. Over and above her own fears, Kathleen was upset that she could not provide any answers or relief for her students. This only increased her feelings of powerlessness. She felt it was her duty to help her students and ease their fears. How could she do this when she herself was in the dark about what was occurring?

Kathleen sent the listserv a troubling email in 2005. The school was informed of a "hit list" created by one of the students. For her, the way the administration handled the incident was more upsetting than the incident itself.

Anyone in the local area see the news tonight? I was late getting home (due to the following circumstances) but understand that they talked about WHS's current violence threats. Don't know how much was mentioned on TV, but I can tell you that it has been a long and stressful day that included approximately 50 cops on campus (as well as an ambulance and fire truck for precaution), the chief of police, and the director of --- County schools. We'll basically be in a lockdown-type situation for the next two days (leading up to our Spring Break) as the police attempt to identify and arrest the students responsible for repeated race-based death threats.

Despite the good ol' boy reputation of WHS, this crisis has totally caught me off guard. A large majority of our students are saddened (as well as scared out of their wits) and upset by the rumors and reactions surrounding this situation. They're as stunned and confused as I am.

What I thought I would share is the faculty's concern, which was repeatedly voiced at the emergency meeting after school. Quite frankly, the administration did a terrible job of informing teachers of the situation. As a matter of fact, we weren't informed of anything until the administration decided to call the entire student body into the gym so that they could speak directly to the students. The most frustrating and stressful part of this entire experience (and this is a common sentiment among the faculty) is that when our students were looking to us for comfort and support, we were utterly abandoned by our administration. Of course, the professionals I work with did their best to comfort students. Still, when you have kids telling you about the thirty cop cars, ambulance, and fire truck in the parking lot and the cops who won't let them go to their lockers (neither which you know anything about), then you've got problems. Let's just hope that administration can put down their defenses long enough to understand the faculty's concerns and attempt to learn something from the situation, which is all I would request. After all, how can they possibly expect us to help curb/ diffuse the problem when they won't even consider informing us?

Kathleen later related during a May 2005 interview:

Nobody was really told about what was going [on]. All we were told is there was issues but nobody told us there was a hit list. Administration didn't tell us the details of anything and then all of a sudden one day, rumors were going around. One day they called an emergency assembly and they took everybody into the gym and they had the 50 cops in the gym and they had the director of schools, the superintendent, and they had the chief of police, and they had all of the principals and all the students came in. They [the students] asked me what are we doing here . . . I didn't have an answer. They hadn't told the teachers anything. They just brought us in. We didn't even know about it at the beginning of block and they just came over the announcements and said everyone in there. Called us in and then got the chief of police telling students that there's lot wrong and they can be taken to court and brought up and they still don't address what the it is or you know what it is that they've found or why students should be scared or shouldn't be scared or what they were doing about it. It was just all this vague kind of, you know, there's something out there . . .

The students were taken aback and some of them were really upset and many left the assembly crying and afraid. The teachers were pretty upset and yet doing their best to keep students calm and in line but pretty upset that we were at the same level as the students. We couldn't really comfort the students with no information whatsoever; there was a sense of disrespect in that we weren't told anything.

Questions for Teacher Educators and Teachers

- What is the role of teacher education programs in situations like this?
- Is there anything that teacher educators can do to prepare candidates for scenes like this? Should it be their job to do so?
- If you are a classroom teacher, have you ever experienced an incident like this? If so, what did your administration do?
- As a teacher, what would be the ideal way for administrators to handle something like this? What amount of information would you like to know?

Questions for Administrators

Unfortunately, there are defining moments, situations, or issues that school leaders will inevitably face. While all the circumstances may not be the same, the magnitude of the situations will be.

- What can school leaders do in a proactive manner to ensure that their faculty/staff are a priority in the communications should a situation emerge?
- Keeping in mind that Kathleen is a novice teacher, what could the administration do in the wake of this incident to debrief new teachers to better help them understand these situations?
- How can administrators, regardless of the situation, keep the faculty/staff from a feeling of abandonment as expressed by Kathleen?

Chapter Six

From School to School and Classroom to Classroom: Permanently Part-Time

Although Mike and I have long been familiar with traveling teachers—those who do not have their own classroom but shuffle from room to room to teach—neither of us had honestly thought much about these short- and long-term teachers and how mentoring and induction relates to them. My first teaching position, other than being a substitute teacher, was for three months when I temporarily replaced a teacher on maternity leave. In many respects, it was an easy job. I taught physical education at my alma mater (note that my background is English). Because I had gone to school there, and knew many of the teachers and administrators, I had little difficulty adjusting to the culture and norms. However, for a teacher not familiar with the school, such a short-term position could have been difficult.

In this chapter Case #11 features Erin, who ended up having five temporary positions in her first year teaching. We only feature three of the placements in this chapter because they point to the need to properly induct and mentor teachers like her, even though they may not be permanently on staff. Erin's story is one for both teacher educators and administrators, and points to the need for support after graduation. She was not initially hired for a full-time job, but rather, had a series of short-and long-term substitute contracts. Erin is truly that silent member of many faculties that we know are there, but we tend to not invest much time and energy in because we know she will be gone in a short time. While it is important to note that the supply positions that Erin served in have clearly contributed to her growth as a teacher, that growth was her own doing and not the result of any local support.

One of the first observations is the negative message she seems to receive from each school. While this is an issue for another chapter dealing with school culture, it is important to note its presence in many first year teachers' experiences. Several of the teachers at these schools conveyed negative messages to her related to the students. For example, in one instance she was told to run, and in another she was informed her that the students' parents cannot read. To a new teacher, information coming from an established, veteran teacher—whether true or not—is often taken as truth.

There is also an instructional issue present in Erin's case. There does not appear to be any oversight or monitoring from the leadership's behalf to ensure that she knows the requirements in the courses she is teaching and the students she serves. Although she is in an interim capacity, teachers such as Erin should still receive the same support, monitoring, and guidance as full-time teachers in order to maintain the instructional integrity of the program.

CASE #11: ERIN

August 11, 2004 (mid-afternoon)

Long sigh of relief
Okay, so for at least the next 9 weeks I'm employed at S--- High School. It could be the whole term, depends how long it takes for this lady's hip to heal. It's a supply position, so no benefits or anything, but it beats the living crap out of subbing and selling retractable awnings. I'll only have one day to get ready, and I won't know til tomorrow what grades I'm going to have. I did my field experience at there so I got to know some of the people. I'm incredibly nervous of course, but I also feel like the giant hippopotamus finally lifted his fat rump off of my chest.

August 11, 2004 (evening)

I've got 10, 11, and 12, all Fundamental. The people seem pretty cool so far, there's lots of laughter and most everyone has been very willing to help. They're treating me like I'm actually part of the faculty and not just a fill-in, which I sincerely appreciate. Another cool thing is that my classes are very small. The other teachers have given me some interesting pointers about dealing with "fundies," as they call them; however, they told me to bring air freshener because "they fart a lot," don't assign homework, don't try to make them write more than twice a week (?!), and speak very slowly. One lady wondered why I was bothering to send home parent letters, since "most of their parents can't read." So I'm a little apprehensive . . . but the anxiety is balanced out by relief; at least until the end of October, I won't be selling retractable awnings from a kiosk at the mall. Maybe this will lead into something less temporary.

September 24, 2004

Hooray for emotional roller coasters. I'm too tired to be eloquent. I'm still pretty sure this is what I want to do, at least until I write the Great American Novel. At inservice today I got to catch up with the people from my internship school and hear how my kids from last year are doing. I'm only here for one more month, then it looks like I'm going to CHS to teach 10 CP [college prep] for the rest of the year, but it's not a definite yet. Being a supply teacher sucks. You have all the responsibilities and paperwork of a normal teacher, but with less money and no benefits.

October 23, 2004

And here's my situation. Last day at SHS, tears, presents. W-- Middle School, starting Tuesday and ending in January, when I will start at CHS, unless the "Fahrenheit 9/11" lady gets dismissed, which is a distinct possibility. In the meantime, my assignment is 7th grade L.A., remedial reading, and social studies. All of the 7th grade teachers are 1st year teachers, because everybody left. The kids scared 'em off. 33 kids in remedial reading, 7th period, and that's the smallest class. As soon as the principal was out of earshot, the other teachers told me, "RUN."

The guy I'm filling in for was hit by a bus about 3 weeks into the school year. They've had a series of subs ever since, no real discipline or structure, they don't even have any grades. In the last week, Science Teacher Guy says he's caught kids trying to pierce themselves in the bathroom, smearing poop on the walls, and pulling knives on each other. The original teacher was apparently laissez-faire and the kids are totally out of control; Mr. Principal Guy wants me to go in there and lay down the law. Pray for me. Thank God it's only 2 months.

October 26, 2004: "It's only two months"

I've got to keep telling myself that, because W-- Middle is hell on earth. I can't say they didn't warn me, but oh-my-freaking-God. The cuteness of 7th graders is hideously deceptive. I have never encountered a more evil species. Tarantulas? Fire-ants? They've got nothing on 7th period remedial reading. Until today I thought I knew what the hell I was doing. I think I managed to teach about 4 kids that the earth has an elliptical orbit today, and that's it. I would give anything for a big, booming voice that could be heard for miles around . . . if anyone has a secret for making psychopathic mutants masquerading as children shut the hell up for five seconds, please enlighten me . . . even my summer school class never made me break down and cry at the end of the day and feel like a total failure . . . after all, they were just one class, and they were SUPPOSED to be the bottom of the barrel. This was just such a shock, even after being warned, aagh bloody hell I don't even want to talk about it.

October 30, 2004

These kids have had absolutely no structure since Day 1, so it's been a huge challenge just establishing daily procedures. I got the best compliment from a little guy this morning; he said, "I hope you stay here and be our teacher the whole year. You keep 'em under control--Mr. N. just let 'em run wild and we didn't learn nothin'!" Precious little brownnoser. I'm starting to feel SO guilty about leaving these guys; I haven't told them yet. I have some of the same kids for 3 different classes, and it seems they're starting to get used to me. Of course, the rottenest apples are all still suspended. When I expressed my qualms about leaving to one of the other teachers, she looked at me like I'd sprouted another head. "If you have any sense at all," she said, "you will take that job and never look back." Which of course I'm going to, but not until I have some sort of structure established for my unfortunate successor. They may be wild Armenians, but they deserve so much better.

November 14, 2004

All these false starts have been a blessing in disguise. At first I was uber-pissed not to have a permanent position, but I'm so grateful for the range of experiences this year has offered me. During my internship, I hated the thought of leaving that one school where I felt so comfortable, but in retrospect, maybe it would be a good idea to bounce the interns around a little. I've now taught 5 of the 6 grades I'm certified to teach (all but 8th), and I've certainly learned more than I did last year about how very different schools can be, even within the same district. That said, I'm immensely relieved to have found a "home" for the rest of the year. I'm nervous, but this will be my fifth "first-day-at-a-new-school," so the jitters aren't nearly so bad. W--S-- was absolute hell, but it has never occurred to me to quit. That school has a toxic atmosphere, and a seventh grade team composed entirely of new teachers who were completely burned out, exhausted, and disillusioned. I don't want that to happen to any of us. It's awful. wish me luck on what will hopefully be my last "first day" of this school year.

November 15, 2004

Day One is going very well so far. Dude I'm replacing is hanging out today, showing me around . . . everyone here is so friendly! And the kids . . . well, I've been warned about 4th period and haven't met them yet, but so far they seem great. I can actually hear myself speak. I've got 2 blocks of 10 CP and 1 of 10 Regular.

January 6, 2005

This is my first semester where I'll have my own classes all to myself for an entire term, so I'm feeling slightly more like a real teacher. I have a collaborative-model class, and one of the kids asked the special ed teacher (who has been teaching since before I was born) if she was MY intern! Go figure. Looking back, I know this year will just be a blur . . . planning for and learning names in 14 new classes in a single school year is just a little excessive. I'm getting to know people and I hope I get to stay here.

Year Two: A Permanent Position

In her second year, and at the last minute, Erin ended up taking a job at an alternative school in another state. As she wrote in mid-August 2005,

The thing at H--HS fell through at the last minute . . . but I am officially the one and only English person in the Second Chance program. I suppose I have a way with delinquents . . . geez, I wonder why . . . I'm not sure entirely what the position entails. I know there are currently only 20 kids, total, in Second Chance, and the hours are bizarro, 11AM-7PM, because we're sharing a building with the alternative center and the middle school program. They actually managed not to lose any of my paperwork, so I should be starting early next week . . . in the meantime, I'm subbing, and working nights and weekends at Steinmart.

FOLLOW-UP

Despite the stresses of working with adolescents who have been in trouble in their previous schools and/or with law enforcement, Erin found her niche. And, the experiences as a part-time teacher provided her with valuable skills in adaptation and classroom management. Later in that year, she sent a humorous email to the group relating the average day teaching.

A Day in the Life of Ms. E., Second Chance English Aficionado

10:30 Show up. Dodge middle schoolers. Get bitched at by Mr. B-- because one of my kids left a paperclip on the floor last night. Hook up laptop, check email, grade yesterday's work, plan for today, put some grades in. If it's Tuesday, attend a meeting, listening to my co-workers bitch about how useless the kids are while I doodle angry bunnies in the margin of my notebook. Assist with intake of new kids and tweak schedule if necessary. Eat breakfast.

1:15 High school kids arrive. Make everyone tuck in shirts, remove headwear, and put away electronic devices. When did everyone get an Ipod suddenly? Is this a conspiracy? Should I get one? Request that D. please not drop his pants in public in order to tuck in his long, pink tee. Herd everyone to their respective homerooms. At this point, P. will ask to use my Visine and/or body spray; I refuse, so he asks someone else, who lets him. It doesn't make him look or smell any less stoned, however. Take attendance.

1:20 First period. Kids get their folders and books, do journals, and pick up wherever they left off in their packets. Help D. with Romeo and Juliet, read a Frost poem to J., brainstorm persuasive topics with A., wake up Q., revoke R.'s computer privileges because he's looking for Asian porn rather than doing research for his travel brochure. Attempt to de-escalate verbal altercation between Y. and S., ask I. to please put his shoes back on.

2:30 Remind everyone where they're supposed to go next; switch and repeat, but insert different initials, assignments, articles of clothing, and varieties of porn.

3:30 Switch again and repeat.

4:20 Lunch. Hide in classroom for fifteen minutes and eat a Slim-Fast bar. A., a.k.a. "Columbine," also hides in my room so the other kids won't beat him up. He spouts rhetoric pertaining to right-wing politics, economics, history, and the Church of Satan while I eat. Y. comes in to borrow a tampon, makes a derogatory comment to A., who smells "musty" today, and disappears for the remainder of the day (if I'm lucky). Mr. D., the prematurely balding science teacher from New Jersey, usually stops in for a minute and participates in semi-intellectual discourse with A. Make sure no crumbs fall on the floor—not that a lack of crumbs is any deterrent for the flourishing ecosystem of vermin in this ancient building. Meanwhile, the odor of Mrs. V.'s Jamaican Jerk Goat dish fills the hallway. This is fitting because Mrs. V. actually is a Jamaican jerk.

4:35 Try desperately, with the aid of the cop, to wrangle everyone out of the break room and into fourth period. Assist custodian in cleanup of microwave-related explosion; prevent Little J. from placing Little B. in the refrigerator or trash can. Due to increased blood sugar, everyone is very hyper during fourth, except Big J., who ate a large potato and is now very sleepy. By the time all this is accomplished, 4th is nearly halfway over.

5:30 Return to homeroom; this is the "advisement" period, although they're expected to do academic work until 6:30. After 6:30, it's impossible to get anyone to do anything. We'll generally sit around and talk about music, current events, pets, gadgets, cars, etc; I try to steer the conversation away from drugs and malicious gossip, and insert applicable life-skills stuff when possible. Sometimes the social worker or some other speaker will come in and do an activity with them.

6:55 Suddenly everyone forgets how to tell time. I deter several escape attempts and remind them that when 7:00 does roll around, they'll be expected to exit through the door rather than the window. Make them straighten up the room and shut down the computers. At 7:00, A. has to be reminded that it's time to go and that he can stop working. Herd everyone out, lock up, and watch them meander down to the MARTA stop, smoking cigarettes and rejoicing loudly as if they've just been released from prison.

And if you think that was long, you should experience the actual day. . . . But yeah, it's really not so bad. I'm in a good mood today.

As of January 2008, Erin was still teaching at the second chance school, and was heavily involved in professional development activities for other teachers. As she wrote,

I actually almost have an area of expertise. Since the last time I spoke to you, my principal and I have presented nationally on the subject of using academic service learning in an alternative school setting. We spoke at the NMSA conference in Houston, and we have been invited to present at two other conferences this year. I have conducted trainings and focus groups for other Learn and Serve schools throughout Georgia.

Erin finally found the support and mentoring to enable her to become the self-confident professional she desired. Ironically, her transient initial entry into the profession—with all the lessons she was forced to learn on her own—made her stronger. Yet, it could have turned out very differently, if not for the guidance of her current administrators.

Questions for Teachers and Teacher Educators

- What can teacher education programs do, if anything, to prepare their candidates for short-term positions such as Erin's?
- What can and should fellow teachers do to assist short-term teachers?
- Do schools need to have formal mentoring programs for these teachers too?

Questions for Administrators

Principals are responsible for recruiting and selecting teachers for their schools. Erin is a prospective candidate for each of these schools in which she teaches during this first year. However, there does not appear to be any localized effort to support her.

- What can school principals do for teachers who are teaching on a short term basis? Should a lead teacher or school administrator be assigned to assist all itinerant teachers?

- How can principals view migratory teachers as prospective teaching candidates for their schools?
- How might have Erin's experiences and perceptions of each school be viewed differently if she were greeted by the principal and had follow-up conferences periodically?

Because Erin does not belong to any school in particular, no person or entity seems to take responsibility for her growth.

- In cases such as this, should the system assume responsibility for ensuring that migratory teachers are supported and guided during their time with the system?

Chapter Seven

Unhealthy Departments

According to recent research on schools, there are five common school culture problems—gossip, problem-saturated conversation, cliques, an "us-them" attitude, and resentment and negativity (Beaudoin & Taylor, 2004). Each of these can take over a school; however, when a few or all of them exist among staff and faculty, new teachers face tremendous difficulty in adapting to and surviving in such a school. For example, gossip in schools creates problems in that it decreases possible collaboration among faculty, which can then lead to teacher isolation. In addition, it creates a negative and distrustful environment where resentments can fester.

It is very easy for new teachers to get caught up in or believe gossip, especially if they do not know anyone at their school before they accept employment there. Beaudoin and Taylor (2004) also note the problems associated with "problem-saturated" conversation, such as its negative drain on energy, can create more gossip among faculty, and can escalate to include talking negatively about students and labeling them. New teachers can also get swept up in negative conversations, especially those about students. I (Lisa) tell my pre-service teachers not to share their class lists with other teachers at the beginning of the year because, inevitably, a colleague will name off all the "bad" students, thus already tainting the teacher's perception of his/her students.

The three remaining culture problems, cliques, an "us-them" attitude, and resentment and negativity, in our experience are intertwined and closely correlated with gossip. For example, cliques, whether they naturally form by department (which seems innocuous) or through out-of-school social activities, can have the same end result: they cut off others in the school from joining or feeling welcome. Feeling disconnected from colleagues can lead to an "us-them" attitude among faculty and lead to resentment and negativity. Once anger and bitterness becomes more prevalent than optimism, positive change is unlikely.

As a new teacher, I faced this in my third teaching position. Going to the faculty break room was like being in high school all over again, with whispering, gossip, and factions holding court. It was high school all over again—with only the cool teachers (whoever the cool teachers were) being allowed to sit at the one table. It caused me and another "new to the school" teacher to split the cost of a microwave so we could eat our lunches together in her room and avoid the break room altogether. Our awkward isolation led to the clique's further disdain. Both of us ended up leaving the school at the end of the first semester.

The cases featured in this chapter center on unhealthy and/or unresponsive departments. While it is unrealistic to expect that everything will go well all the time and that department members will be "one big happy family," new (and veteran) teachers should expect to be treated kindly and with respect. Case #12 concerns Toni, who was frustrated over not being mentored or taken care of by her colleagues and administrators during her first year in the classroom. She felt ignored and isolated and came to realize that good students could not compensate for the icy school culture she faced on a daily basis. This, ultimately, cause her departure.

Kasey and Dan, the teachers in Case #13, did not work with colleagues as unfriendly as Toni. However, working with virtual strangers for a year, also took its toll on them: both left at the end of the first year and moved back home. Because of their novice status, all three teachers were afraid to say anything outside of their online support group, in fear of making conditions worse, so they suffered in silence, only vocalizing the problems to the listserv members.

CASE #12: TONI'S STORY

Toni's story will resonate with many novice teachers, and even some veteran teachers (like me) who change schools during their career (see Scherff, 2008 for fuller story). The truth is this: some schools, and departments within schools, are unfriendly. For whatever reason, faculty members are unkind and can even be outwardly hostile to teach other (but especially to new teachers). Toni says that she later found out that her department had a reputation for being unkind and that someone finally told her the truth. I spoke to a teacher who taught in that department four years prior and she verified Toni's story—teachers in the department were cold, sometimes mean, and not prone to collaboration. Learning this after the fact was more painful than if she had known the working climate at the time of her interview. Perhaps if her fellow teachers were more open and helpful, Toni might have had enough support to get through the stressful times. Perhaps she would not have quit halfway through her second year. Perhaps she would not have accepted the position at all.

Immediately after graduating from the master's program, Toni was offered a position at a local high school with a good reputation. Teachers in the district earn quite a bit more per year than their counterparts in neighboring areas. With school about to start, Toni was spending time preparing her room and initial lessons. She was also looking forward to meeting her new colleagues and learning about her responsibilities.

The first issue she encountered was indifferent colleagues. Toni sought friends in her department only to find herself ignored. Only three weeks into the school year Toni closed an e-mail with, "I guess my only real concern at this point is that at school I feel utterly alone." Later, in September, she reiterated this point writing to the group, "oh, and someone finally told me the truth . . . that my English department was 'known' for being unkind and hateful. Great! Well, I guess that explains a few things." Even though Toni eventually came to terms with the atmosphere in her department, she was never really able to work past it. "I don't think I am going to be able to get over not having friends in the department I teach with. It's just not normal, not cool."

Toni's understanding of what good induction and mentoring should look like made her situation worse. As a novice teacher, Toni sought the collaboration and discussion that took place the year before among her fellow student teachers and between her and her mentors. Knowing how valuable and enriching those conversations were, to be missing them now, was even more detrimental. Toni was quite clear in describing the conditions that hampered her experience.

It's so obvious to me. From having classes with you and others; it's been so obvious what should have happened here. I should have had a great experience. I shouldn't have been given the worst classes, all those things that research shows that new teachers need, or just a general good experience, not just being thrown to the wolves . . . if teachers were eased in, given lots of support, felt that they were given classes they'd be good at and not what no one else wanted to teach that they would last longer . . . cause otherwise, my first year's been so frustrating that at Christmas I was contemplating quitting . . . not right then but at the end of the year . . . . It just seems like it's still traditional. No one takes it to heart what new teachers need.

Despite her negative first year experience, Toni was more hopeful about her second year. Yet, her confidence had been shaken and she was plagued with feelings of self-doubt. Statements like, "I'm looking forward to actually feeling like a good teacher again next year" were distressing. Looking back at our interview, she offered foreshadowing of what was to come: "If it doesn't happen for me and it's another year like this, then I won't be back. And, if it's some kind of crazy schedule, I'm sorry but I'm not going to do it . . . hopefully that won't happen because I'll definitely feel like a failure. I already do."

Although the summer provided some mental and emotional relief for Toni, hearing about a fellow listserv member's decision to leave the profession and look for a job that was more satisfying prompted her to consider other career options. By mid-September, seeing no improvement in sight, she e-mailed me (Lisa) about her situation: "Our new principal is less than desirable. I couldn't feel any worse about leaving, but I have to reason that thirty days should be most adequate for most any job. I can't help that teaching is the way it is. I feel like if I do not leave I will suffer a serious personal catastrophe in the near future."

She announced her decision to resign to listserv members a month later and after her last day of teaching wrote " . . . I'm walking away. I'm walking away from all the time I spent in school, all the files and supplies I have, many sweet students, health insurance, all of it. Teaching is just not worth the constant stress and pain that crushed my very soul and being." The following year she reflected on the experience:

After reading over my e-mails I just want to cry out "why are you driving us away!?" Why have you left us alone, fending for ourselves among a sea of IEPs, screaming students, angry parents, micromanaging superiors, and unfeeling co-workers? Here we are, stripped of our sense of purpose. Our plans trampled. I remember sitting on my husband's lap practically yelling about all the great plans I had. This year was going to be great! I knew my stuff, I had files, I had plans, I had experience. I could handle it! And if it didn't work out, we would find a new job for me the next year. Instead, I'm looking for a job now.

LISA AND MIKE'S ANALYSIS

Every principal knows the dynamics of his/her school and its faculty. In Toni's case, there appears to be a department that has secured its own personality. Toni is entering the school and the department leaving behind the securities of the university and the internship. In Toni's story the department that should have embraced her and assisted her transition, appears to have made no formal or informal effort to do so. Toni demonstrates those traits of successful teachers; she is energetic, analytical, and extremely organized. It appears that these very traits are what prevent her from being able accept and operate in the climate of the department.

Like many new teachers, Toni is hesitant to ask for help. It is often the mindset of the new teacher that reaching out to co-workers and supervisors in a sign of weakness. Toni states, "I'm also scared to ask for help with something too because I don't want to seem incompetent." Like in most schools, principals and teachers don't have enough time in the day to accomplish all of their goals and responsibilities. While this demand exists, it is necessary for them to reach out and inquire to the needs of new teachers.

While Toni's perception of her department is negative, it is possible that it is only her perception. New teachers are forced to make judgments about co-workers in a short period of time. It is possible that Toni misjudged her department and the individuals in the department; however, because she did not have a support system in place, there was no opportunity to adjust those impressions and judgments. Without proper guidance from the school, Toni is forced to forge her own opinions of people and the school which have a drastic impact on her deliberation whether to remain at the school and in the profession.

Toni seems unaware of the expectations placed on her as a teacher in the school other than her own desire to teach. In education we often assume we know the roles, responsibilities, and expectations for teachers. However, in Toni's case, a more detailed review of her job description and expectations from the onset may have proven helpful. In many cases during the dialogue, Toni is forced to make her own determinations of her job performance:

> *I'm scared I won't measure up, but I am unwilling to do any more than I'm doing-surviving. If they don't like me they can say "adios" it's their decision. I just don't know how understanding they're going to be when they apparently don't have many new first-year teachers. I don't know how I compare to the other teachers either, but they are all so much more experienced than me that I must look like a fool.*

While Toni most likely participated in a formal teacher evaluation system, it appears that she was not getting the feedback she needed to encourage her continued growth. Toni is placed in her classroom with little direction and feedback; therefore, she seems to begin to sense her inadequacies as weaknesses in her ability to teach. There is a good chance that the same difficulties that Toni is experiencing with students are the same that a teacher across the hall may be experiencing, but there is no system in place to allow Toni to recognize this.

Questions for Teachers and Teacher Educators

- If you are working in a department like Toni's, what would you do?
- If you were Toni's department head, what should/could you have done?
- What can teacher educators do to prepare their pre-service teachers for conditions such as this?
- How much do you think school administrators knew about the department's climate? If they knew of its reputation, why was nothing done?
- If administrators didn't know, what about the school's culture prevented department members from talking to the administration about the problems?
- What can principals do to make sure that future "Toni's" do not occur?

Questions for Administrators

- In Toni's case, how could a mentor have served as an in-house person to assist transition Toni into the school and the culture of the school?
- If Toni had someone to bounce these ideas and feelings off of on a consistent basis, might she have been transitioned into understanding her niche in the department?
- How could a mentor have assisted her in understanding the tacit operations of the school and the department, therefore providing more insight and a better understanding?
- What formal methods can principals put into place to elicit the needs of new teachers?
- Would a monthly meeting with the principal and Toni have been an opportunity for such dialogue? If so, how could those meetings have been structured?
- Assuming the principal in Toni's school knew about the department's history, how could he/she have formally introduced Toni into this setting in a protected and nourishing manner?
- Instead of Toni being immersed in the department's unsupportive climate, how might the principal have arranged for a support network during this transition?
- If this climate exists and the principal is aware of it, should he/she inform Toni of the department's strengths and weaknesses during the interview?
- Could a department meeting welcoming Toni have been an appropriate method of induction into the department?
- What other methods could the principal have employed to send the message to the department the importance of supporting a new teacher?

CASE #13: KASEY AND DAN

Sea Spray High School appears to have the opportunity to recruit and retain Kasey and Dan. They are thrilled about teaching, they love the location, and they are prepared to teach. At first, teaching and working in the school were going fine. There does appear to be some attempt by the leadership of the school to induct the new teachers into the school. Dan appreciates the principal's desire to welcome the new teachers as he tells the story of the principal lining up all the new teachers and having the other 70 teachers introduce themselves to each new teacher. This event was exciting for Dan because the principal recognized the need to welcome the large group of new teachers. Unfortunately, this is the only event of this nature that Dan provides.

Moreover, the school culture does little else to induct them into the profession. Dan discusses an online required course that is forced and of little positive impact. Dan expresses the importance of being surrounded by caring colleagues when he discusses the impact that the department head has on his entrance to the school. His identification of a caring individual is of great importance to him and the judgments he places on his new school. It seems that if the department in this case continued the welcome they provided at the first of the year throughout the year, they could have retained two teachers.

Knowing the priorities and concerns of new teachers entering a school and the profession is critical to a school and its leadership. Inducting new teachers is not the role of the principal or mentor alone. Grade level teachers or department level teachers have an organizational role in welcoming new professionals. Unfortunately, Dan and Kasey do not have the organizational support that is needed for new teachers. This lack of support from the department has a profound impact on the success of students and new teachers alike. For example, Kasey and Dan are forced to identify the state standards on their own with little direction from the department, principal, or system. Dan and Kasey require professional support from their colleagues similar to what they were provided with in their preparation program. It is harmful for schools to assume that novices no longer need such support once they exit their preparation program.

Small things mean a lot to new teachers. Every action or inaction is a message sent to them. While the example of Dan sharing the room with another teacher seems to be an issue of logistics alone, to Dan it becomes a strong message that he should not interfere with the pre-existing culture. In a most polite way, he is told to make himself at home so long as he does not overstay his welcome in the room. He is merely a guest. Dan enters this profession excited about teaching and impacting students' successes, yet this is how he is embraced as a new professional. The power of a classroom space can also be seen in Kasey's excitement for her portable. She states, "It's amazing how much potential you can see in a trailer or dry erase boards. I felt like this was my vessel that I could use to change my kids." Unfortunately, the room for new teachers becomes the one place that they can retreat to when the rest of the school isolates them. Common in secondary settings, teachers often teach in isolation with little opportunity to engage in collegial opportunities to grow as professionals.

Early on, Dan found an advocate in his department head, relating a story to the group (August 7):

The teacher I am sharing with has the room for two periods just like I have them for two periods, but maybe because she's been here before, she seems to think that it is her room. She moved all her stuff into the room, I'm talking teacher's desk, cloth patterned scrapbooks, HER OWN computer, and a whole bunch of books from her old classroom. Along with that she brought three of those long, non-collapsible tables!! I had to move my own desk in there, so the room has thirty student desks, two teacher desks, a computer desk and THREE TABLES!! Now, in her defense, she's been very "I want you to feel like this is your room, too," in all our conversations, but she's was also pretty consistent in recommending that I use a desk and the computer in the teacher's lounge. Well, until I told her that the dept. head said I could move the desk into the room. I love my department head. She came looking for me, and she discovered what the woman had done to the room. My dept. head was furious about the excess tables, and the fact that these books should no longer be in her possession. She was also angry that the sharing teacher left me no space on the bookcase and was clearly taking over the room as if it were her own. As I said before, I love my department head. I told her that I don't want to start anything or get any negative vibes going on, but I definitely was feeling pushed out. She agreed, and felt she could handle the situation diplomatically since the teacher has books she is not supposed to have. I don't want any bad business going on between me and the other teacher, but it feels good to know that you have people who will stand behind you if there is trouble. I just hope this does not create tension between the two of us.

Whether due to the multiple demands placed upon teachers and department heads or someone being on his or her best behavior at the beginning of the year, this initial, supportive effort was short-lived. Kasey and Dan never mentioned their department head or colleagues in their emails to the group for the rest of that first year. However, in their end-of-the-year interview, they both had much to say about those they worked with. When asked to describe the culture of their department the words they used were: "friendly," "neutral," "unsupportive," "inward," "apathetic," and "very independent and focused independently."

While their department head fixed the shared classroom situation, it appears that support faded away after that. Department meetings should be spaces where curriculum is discussed, lessons are shared, and teachers support one another. However, at Sea Spray, department meetings seem to be nothing more than obligatory time together.

One of the biggest frustrations for both teachers was the lack of guidance in terms of state standards that needed to be taught. Coming from another state, neither Kasey nor Dan were familiar with Florida's language arts standards. No one in the department, it seemed, was willing or interested in helping them learn what they needed to teach and how or when, even when curricular issues should have been discussed, such as in department meetings. Kasey and Dan related this fact in their interviews.

> Dan: *We all get together and say a few things and then that was it. I never saw anything good pretty much past that . . . it basically comes down to there seems to be a certain group that functions independently and does so very well, but does not realize what the whole means.*

> Kasey: *There's no program where you sit down with other teachers who are going to teach what you're gonna teach and get any ideas. It was like, "here's the book." "Teach juniors." "Have a good time." You have to go to them and be like, "Hey, have you taught juniors? Okay. Help me out here." It wasn't like the sophomore teachers ever get together and discuss anything. The junior teachers never get together and discuss anything. We were first year teachers and they were just kind of like, "Here's the book. Have a good time. Teach whatever you want to teach." So, that was irritating that literally, there was no support. It was like the support where you needed it wasn't there but all the other stuff where you didn't really need it, it was kind of piled on.*

Another aspect of their department that was hard for them to accept was what they perceived as a lack of camaraderie or concern. Like other novice teachers, Kasey and Dan came from a teacher education program that fostered collegiality and an atmosphere of care and trust through its cohort model. Because the student teachers took their courses together and had an online support network as they progressed through the final months of their program, entering schools where colleagues did not talk was a difficult adjustment. When asked about her department, this is what Kasey had to say: "I really don't know them that well to be honest . . . I like Miss__ even though we we've had some run-ins . . . I like most of them. Sometimes they're not very supportive, I guess [sighs]. How do I say it? The department head . . . usually he's in a hurry to get the meetings [done]. So that's one thing . . . but the department, in general . . . I don't really know them that well actually." My response was, "After a year?"

Kasey did not seem as upset over the departmental snubbing as Toni, and she attributed this to having Dan there to support her. However, she did add that "I guess the point is you do have to go and ask them. It's not like they're not knocking on your door saying Hi, how are you doing? Are you, you know, do you need anything? It's not like that." Dan, on the other hand, felt more resentment towards his colleagues because of their action (or inaction). He was particularly troubled over their lack of support for Kasey during a department meeting.

When Kasey's article came out . . . One of the teachers was flipping through it [English Journal] and noticed that it was written by someone, from our university, and of course so he saw her name and made a statement about it and it was kind of like, "Yay." And afterwards nobody said a word to her about it. It wasn't even like, "Wow, that's great that you actually, you know, something you said and did was actually published." She didn't even want anybody to know about it cause she knew that was what the reaction was gonna be. The teacher who discovered her name was asking her some questions. When she was trying to talk it was kind of like they all had ADD and just zoned out completely and didn't even listen. And, of course, the department head was like, "Yeah, that's great" and then just kind of blew it off.

That's what I meant by unsupportive and apathetic; every meeting we get together, we sit there. There are certain people that get what they want every time and other people who don't pretty much are ignored or not seen. It's almost like it's a power struggle between them , who knows what and has what and who teaches what. Of course it's typical that the older teachers or the teachers that have been here longer are always the ones that they get the honors students, they get the IB kids and, of course, the new teachers are left with everything else. I don't know, I think that's really just not a good way to do things, especially if you want new teachers to stick around. You should give them at least one class of students that are actually self-motivated cause it would at least make them feel better about their entire experience.

Questions for Teachers and Teacher Educators

- Who bears the burden for this situation? Kasey and Dan? Why or why not?
- What could they have said or asked of their department chair, fellow English teachers, and/or administrators?
- Who should they have talked to?
- Knowing that they didn't talk to anyone at their school, what prevented them?
- Should anyone, especially administrators, have known what was going on?

- Is it the principal's responsibility to deal with departmental issues such as this? Or, are they just the status quo?
- How can teacher education programs more effectively prepare teachers to work with and interact with their department members?

Questions for Administrators

- Dan and Kasey willingly reach out for support and assistance from their listserv peers. How could the principal have organized a similar system of support for them in the school?
- Could a mentor serve as the facilitator during their induction?
- Should the department head have served in a more formal role in their induction?
- How can principals survey new teachers periodically to ensure that they are being supported from their peers?
- At Sea Spray High School, approximately thirty new teachers were hired. How can the principal provide individual support for such a large number of new teachers?
- While individual support is needed, the support of the department is also needed. How can school leaders work with departments, teams, or grade levels to ensure that they serve as a support network for a new teacher?
- In the case of Dan and Kasey, could a portion of each department meeting be allocated to the needs of new teachers?
- How might a course of study alignment guide relieve much of the burden that these two professionals felt coming into the school?
- How does a principal lead a department to understand its organizational responsibility in supporting new teachers?
- Furthermore, how might have the veteran teachers grown from collegial interactions with Kasey and Dan?

As schools continue to experience rapid growth, it becomes necessary to share spaces in schools, especially at the secondary level.

- What can school leaders do to ensure that sharing classroom space does not serve as a barrier to the success of a new teacher?
- As it relates to Dan, what could the principal have done to ensure that the room sharing arrangement was done in a positive manner?
- How could have the classroom sharing experience be turned into one of support and growth for Dan?

Chapter Eight

The Faculty Lounge

Many difficulties that novice teachers encounter often stem from their need—or inability—to adjust to the organizational customs of the school and to its stakeholders (Shulman, 1987). All schools have their own histories that exist before teachers come to them (Craig, 1999) and new teachers must immediately engage in dialogue and mediate behavior in the macro-and micro-contexts already established (Rex & Nelson, 2004). Regarding school culture, there are both informal and formal structures. Informal structures include the day-to-day processes (i.e., how things get accomplished); formal structures include the school's governing system and articulated expectations (Brock & Grady, 2001).

Related to these are two significant components of an organization's culture: norms and assumptions. Norms are the principles that a school institutionalizes and sanctions—the acceptable and unacceptable. Assumptions are things which are unspoken but acknowledged as correct and nonnegotiable (Brock & Grady, 2001). Hart and Bredeson (1996) denote four levels of school culture—those cultural elements common to schools in general, those characteristic of a particular school, those shared by a specific kind of school, and those unique to the people who make up the school community.

The effect of a school's environment is one critical variable to discuss when assessing early teaching experiences (Flores & Day, 2006). Beginning teachers enter the field from teacher education programs where there is often freedom to make decisions, climates that are open to discussion and collaboration, and conditions that nurture personal relationships. In the schools they often run into a set of norms and behaviors that clash with their experiences (Feiman-Nemser & Buchman, 1987; Flores & Day, 2006; Sabar, 2004). Novice teachers engage in a struggle trying to create their own social realities by "attempting to make their work match their personal vision of how it should be, whilst at the same time being subjected to the powerful socializing forces of the school culture" (Day, 1999, p. 59).

Weiss (1999) found that beginning teachers' views of the social organization of their schools, including leadership and culture, were the variables most closely related to morale, commitment, and planned retention. She found that second-year teachers who had completed one-year internships in schools that were structurally responsive to their needs were more prone to feel the harmful impact of non-collaborative cultures or unsupportive school leadership (Weiss, 1999). Kuzmic (1994) adds, "Without some basic understanding of the organizational life of schools . . . beginning teachers may be ill-equipped to deal with the problems and difficulties they encounter or develop the political tactics and teaching strategies needed to resist" (p. 24).

When we were high school students, the teachers' lounge was a mysterious place. Once in a while we students would get a peek inside, but none of us ever dared to venture in. When Mike and I began teaching we realized that, depending on the school, the teachers' lounge could be one of three things: a welcoming spot where colleagues could talk about the events of the day, a depressing no man's land with one old couch and a dried up plant or two, or a smaller version of the high school cafeteria complete with cliques, stares, and whispers.

When teachers, especially those new to a school, find the teachers' lounge an unwelcoming place, then they won't risk going back in fear of being ostracized or ignored. Instead, they will stay in their classrooms, and become even more isolated and alone than they might already feel. In Case #14, Kasey, finds out about the unwritten policies of the teachers' lounge. While the case itself is short, it speaks volumes about how school culture can cause rifts between and among colleagues and alienate new teachers. In two related stories also included in the case, we learn how other novices were similarly introduced to faculty and the school culture.

Each of the three teachers, Kasey, Rachel, and Susan, experiences some form of "faculty lounge" culture at their respective schools. Kasey unknowingly breaks a tacit rule about who could sit where, and when, in the teachers' lounge. Teachers, like everyone else, are creatures of habit—often parking in the same spot every morning, eating at the same table, or lounging on the same couch at the same time every day. Is this right? Maybe not. But, it is the nature of any organization. Another colleague was nice enough to let Kasey know that several teachers were upset: the math group that she sat at their table and one individual teacher who seemingly "owned" couch privileges. Kasey is justified in her frustration that leaves her, and the rest of the teachers, nowhere to sit and eat or rest. Essentially, the faculty lounge is becoming (or has already become) a space for some teachers to utilize more than others, in essence, almost leaving particular teachers with no place to go.

No place to go is exactly where Rachel is left. Her school, due to lack of space, turned the teachers' lounge into a special education classroom thus leaving teachers on one side of the campus with no place to relax. As Rachel laments, because she is in a portable classroom, she is even farther away from the main building; there is nowhere for her to go to talk to other teachers. The situation almost forces her to isolate herself in her classroom and she finds it easier—and more "relaxing"—to eat lunch in her room alone and find any solace in there, too. This imposed segregation adds to her stress and turned out to be a major reason for her unhappiness in the profession.

Kasey and Rachel's school culture are remarkably different from Susan's where teachers are valued, supported, and appreciated by students, parents, and administrators. Each week the teachers are made to feel as if what they do is important. And, that level of support is what helps Susan get through that first tough transition year. She experiences the same job stress, student frustrations, and negative moments just like everybody else, but knowing that she is valued and made to feel special, make her feelings of efficacy much higher.

CASE #13: DON'T SIT ON THE COUCH

Kasey, like most first year teachers, is working to understand her new profession. She appears to look for acceptance and support from her colleagues as a new professional. The message sent to her from the faculty lounge is not a very welcoming one. She is physically isolated in her classroom with children for a predominant portion of her day, so she looks at the faculty lounge as a place where she can let her guard down, rest, and engage in adult conversation.

What Kasey quickly realizes is that the lounge is not the place for this. She is exposed to tacit rules that govern the lounge and the space within it. She also learns that her new peers, whom she most likely looked up to as she entered the school, appear to have established their own hierarchy within the school. These experiences send clear messages to this new teacher. Kasey will be forced to make some decisions. Will she decide to stay in the profession and operate within the school politics? Will she search for collegial support by going to another school or leaving the profession altogether? Below is her original email and some responses from the support group:

Kasey

Ahh, yes, the infamous teachers' lounge. I have third block planning, which is great because that's when all of the lunch periods are. Well, there are couches in the lounge, and I usually end up laying on the couch, sometimes falling asleep among friends. At first, it was hinted at that I probably needed to move from the table because the math people come in the last lunch break and take up most of the table. Okay, that's how I ended up on the couch. Well, one day, one of my friends whispered to me that someone made a comment about me hogging the couch. The comment was made by one of the group that comes in about 20 minutes before my planning period is over. I usually lay on the couch for about 5 or 10 minutes after they come in, wait for Dan, and then we go out to my portable. So, first I needed to move myself and my stuff so math people could eat. Now I'm hogging the couch. So I get up every day and sit next to my friend LeeAnne. The prick who complained about me being a couch hog has yet to sit on the damn couch. Yep, we're still in high school alright!

From: Erin
To: The Group
Subject: Re: Don't sit on the couch

If I were you, Kasey, I'd sprawl out all spread-eagledy on that couch, take off your shoes, have Dan drag in an ottoman and have him feed you grapes. Check under the cushions for change, and if you find any, buy yourself a Coke with it. Round up some palm fronds and tell the math punks they can fan you if they want to. People are so petty.

From: Lane
Subject: Re: Don't sit on the couch

Seriously, I agree with Erin. What pricks! How old are we again? It would be hilarious if you just made it your home from now on. Maybe you could bring in an afghan, one of those doily kinds. Bring in one of your pillows from home and a stuffed animal perhaps. Hang some pictures over the couch, and prop up a few picture frames and candles on a nearby table. Something that really marks your territory, except without peeing around the couch. Of course, if you want to completely alienate your "colleagues" I suppose this method wouldn't be so effective. I don't understand why people are so rude, but I guess the "kill them with kindness" strategy works fairly well.

Kasey learned one implicit and unwritten rule early on: although not formally assigned, some "spaces" belong to particular people (and she also learned that some faculty members can be mean and rude). She learned that not all furniture in the teachers' lounge can be shared. While a humorous tale, it speaks to the culture of a school and how small things can add up to discourage teachers from ever leaving their rooms.

Rachel

Compared to other teachers, Kasey is lucky to have a teachers' lounge at all. At Rachel's high school, administrators turned the teachers' lounge into a class-room due to lack of space. Thus, teachers at her school had nowhere to go outside of their classrooms and the lunchroom. Such conditions are not conducive to forming any kind of community of care among faculty and staff.

Rachel's experience is becoming the norm in many rapidly growing schools and systems. Schools are finding ways to accommodate rapid growth and development which usually means transforming otherwise intended spaces into classrooms. Teaching is already a profession of individual isolation, so when common teacher areas get utilized for instructional spaces there is a good chance it will impact the professional support networks and conversations that can take place within such spaces. Teachers rely on each moment in the day to seek professional conversation from peers. They utilize time in between classes, before and after school, and time spent in common areas as chances to elicit ideas from each other, exchange information, and seek professional guidance on specific issues.

Common professional spaces such as the faculty lounge, if done properly, can be spaces that teachers go to with the intent of getting professional guidance from their peers. The unintended message that Rachel may experience from not having these spaces is that the school does not prioritize collegiality and professional networks. While the space demands for schools take priority, there are other means by which leaders can work to not eliminate the benefits of professional dialogue that may result from common spaces.

We don't even have a break room. The teachers' lounge is turned into a class-room, so we have no [space], there's nowhere for [us to go]. There is one in the social studies wing, but there's not really anywhere for teachers to go, you know, [to] sit on a comfy couch, get some coffee, or anything like that, and talk to each other. There's no place for that. They did turn the teachers' lounge into a special ed [room for] one of the special ed classes. So I eat my lunch in my room. I stay in my room during my planning period; I don't really talk to many people during the day.

The situation at Rachel's school inhibits—and prohibits—teachers from talking to each other, collaborating, and feeling like they are members of a professional community. How are teachers supposed to get some down time or stress relief when there is no space that is their own? After learning more about the working conditions, it was not surprising to hear that morale was extremely low among the faculty and staff. Rachel's situation appears even more poignant when juxtaposed with Susan's.

Susan

Susan's case is one that exemplifies the positives of common spaces such as a faculty lounge. Like many new teachers, she seeks a place where she can share information and seek support. In her case, she is able to see the total support from colleagues and parents alike. The message is clear in Susan's case: the school community recognizes the challenges of teaching and is grateful for the work that the teachers do. It is amazing to see how these positive messages impact Susan's ability to balance the frustrations she has with teaching. Instead of assuming defeat, Susan appears to have developed a stronger determination to work through the daily challenges she faces.

Susan took at job in a suburb of Atlanta and, from the start, was made to feel like a valued professional. As her email below (written in response to Kasey's faculty lounge situation) shows, teachers were frequently made to feel appreciated.

The best thing about my school is the food! We have the best PTA and student council. We have raffles and free prizes every Friday. The PTA provides food (good shit) for all of our staff meetings. At least once a month someone provides breakfast. I'm not talking doughnuts and coffee ---- I'm talking doughnuts, coffee, tea, milk, 5 types of juice, a variety of bagels, doughnuts, cakes, muffins, eggs, chicken sandwiches from Chick-Fil-A, breakfast sandwiches...............you name it, they serve it! Mind you that we have over 300 teachers, and there is AL-WAYS stuff to take home! The PTA and student council even bring shit around on a cart for you in the middle of the day with notes and smiley faces and stuff.

LISA AND MIKE'S ANALYSIS

If there is one thing we have learned from our own experiences with new teachers like Kasey, Rachel, and Susan, it is that if they are not enjoying their job, they will leave. In the past the profession seems to have latched on to the idea of having to deal with certain issues, but stick with your job and school. We have seen all too often with newer teachers, they are not willing to sacrifice their own happiness for their profession. While they are dedicated and compassionate about their roles as teachers, they are not willing to tolerate certain environmental issues. These three cases exemplify this. These three cases also highlight the importance of space in schools and organizations. The use or misuse of space in a school has a tremendous impact on the school culture.

Each of these cases is about the message or the messages that spaces in schools send to teachers. With effective leadership, common spaces in schools can send positive messages and provide new teachers with an informal support network comprised of peers. It is in spaces such as this where powerful dialogue can take place that can support a new professional more than any formal system.

Questions for Teachers and Teacher Educators

- How do we prepare pre-service teachers for conditions like those Kasey and Rachel faced without scaring them away from the profession?
- Who would want to enter a job where there is not a single space to commune—or even eat with—one's colleagues?
- Do we owe it to pre-service teachers to tell them about the harsh realities that they might face when they enter the teaching profession?
- What can colleagues do to assist beginning teachers (and those experienced teachers that change schools) negotiate the common spaces in a school?
- In Kasey's case, is such territorial behavior a form of bullying or just a minor issue?

Questions for Administrators

- What is the school leader's role in ensuring positive common spaces?
- How can school leaders ensure that faculty lounges reflect the type of positive culture they attempt to have in the school?
- In the case of Kasey above, how might the school leader work to break down the negatives that have been created over time?
- In the case of Rachel, how can school leaders maintain the positives of the faculty lounge and other such common spaces as these spaces become utilized for instructional purposes?
- What can school leaders do to create faculty lounges as positive spaces where professional dialogue takes place and where colleagues support each other?
- Is there a place for the principal in the faculty lounge?
- If these spaces can be used to impact the culture of the school, what strategies might principals use to make sure new teachers have a positive experience as they enter the school?

Chapter Nine

Lowering Expectations for Special Education Students

"This whole IEP thing is really worrying me too; can't these parents sue if they find out I'm not treating little Timmy according to his IEP? And if it's not an IEP, it's a 504"—Toni

Does Toni's concern sound familiar? It does for us. I (Lisa) can remember getting bullied by the parents of a special education student during my third year as a teacher. I had heard the horror stories regarding the parents from other teachers—how they had threatened to sue a series of teachers from the elementary grades on up. Then it was my turn. Armed with their thick notebook of what they and their son were entitled to, the parents essentially told me that if their son got picked on in the halls while changing classes and he lashed out and hit another student, it would be my fault and they would take the appropriate legal action. I calmly told the parents that while I understood their concern, I could not leave my classroom to follow their son while he changed classes. Additionally, I informed them that if their son chose to assault another student, he would face the appropriate disciplinary action. Luckily, my principal supported me and the parents backed down. I didn't hear from them again for the remainder of the school year.

Similar anxieties over how to teach and relate to special education students were a recurring theme among the novice teachers. Despite the fact that they had taken a special education class during their teacher preparation program, the teachers felt unprepared for the number of special education students in their classes and the range of accommodations and modifications needed. However, for a few of the teachers, we discovered that the chief issue appeared to be lack of support from both the special education department (and teachers) and school administrators. Feeling like they were forced to compromise their standards nearly led two teachers to quit the profession over the issue. Several teachers felt pressure from their administrators to go over and above special education students' Individual Education Plans (IEPs) and just "pass them along." With the prevalence of inclusion classes, their stories are important for all readers.

In this chapter, the format is slightly different. We present several cases and anecdotes from Lisa, Dave, Shawn, Erin, and Kathleen, followed by our analyses and questions at the end.

CASE #15: REACTIONS AND RESPONSES TO SPECIAL EDUCATION DEMANDS

We're Basically Being Bullied

Lisa entered teaching after a career in the business sector. Towards the end of her first year teaching, she relayed her frustration over what she perceived as a lack of accountability for special education students and special education teachers. The dialogue below is from our May 2005 interview. To differentiate between us, her responses are in italics.

Lisa: *The bureaucracy of dealing with special education is what's driving me crazy. There's just so many things that are done here, and in fact some of the other English teachers have talked about it, too . . . They're doing the kids a disservice because we're just passing these kids when they do not deserve to pass and we're not even giving them a chance to pass, but we're being basically being bullied into passing some of these kids who do not deserve to pass.*

Lisa S.: *Who's bullying?*

Lisa: *Special education.*

Lisa S.: *Why are they? Why are you having to pass them when they don't deserve it?*

Lisa: *Because special education, some of the special education administrators are afraid of lawsuits . . . even with an IEP, when we follow the IEP they're so afraid of lawsuits that we're having to bend over backwards for these kids . . . and have them pass even when they do not deserve to pass, even when a kid won't do anything . . . we're still having to pass them. That's been really, really disturbing to me cause I don't think it's fair to the other kids and it goes against everything I believe in.*

Lisa S.: *Is it isolated to this school or is maybe a district policy?*

Lisa: *I don't know. I'm thinking maybe the school but I don't really know for sure. I know it's been an issue and the principal's aware of it. In fact there was a meeting earlier this week but I couldn't attend cause I had something else going*

on, where they're trying to address some of these issues with special education
cause it's just not working, what we're doing now.

When she returned for the 2005–2006 school year, Lisa found that things
did not improve. As she wrote in an e-mail to me, "As you and I discussed this
summer . . . I'm aggressively trying to find something else to do, especially
since a psycho special education kid vandalized my car and threatened me.
As luck would have it, after numerous attempts to have him removed (by a
school officer), nothing has happened. I've even informed one of the principals that he really scares me."

Lisa continued to struggle with the balance between meeting IEP plans
and maintaining high academic standards in her class for all students. When
another teacher emailed the group about his issues with some special education teachers, Lisa responded,

> *I'm with you on 'dumbing down' the curriculum. Eighteen of my 29 regular*
> *students are failing because I refuse to let them breeze through. I get the impres-*
> *sion that they've been allowed to breeze through . . . until now. In fact, I've got*
> *several disgruntled parents as well as special education teachers because I will*
> *not give them the test answers or give them an A just for writing a paper.*

As we were in the process of writing this book, Lisa sent us a written reflection
on special education, as it was handled at her school. Out of teaching for more
than two years, she is still upset over what happened. The full text is below.

> *I learned a great deal about politics while teaching "lower-level" (regular)*
> *students in a rural high school. Much of my frustration within the public school*
> *system was the manner in which special education students were treated and*
> *the way that administrators handled those concerns. As a new teacher, I was*
> *assigned very low-ability, low-motivated students. Many of my students were*
> *simply biding their time until they reached 18 and could drop out of school. My*
> *classes averaged 25 students, with approximately 7 special education students*
> *in each. The school mainstreamed the special education students; however, the*
> *special education teacher was supposed to work with regular education teach-*
> *ers to ensure that all special education requirements and IEPs were followed.*
>
> *The school principal ordered the special education teacher to plan with each*
> *regular education teacher; however, I rarely saw the special education teacher.*
> *She was supposed to pull individual students to give them assignments and ad-*
> *minister tests in accordance with their IEPs. Whenever she remembered to come*
> *to my classroom, she would storm in and demand that students "come with her*
> *to take tests." This happened every week until I told her that my students were*
> *extremely embarrassed to be called out in front of their peers. In fact, one of*
> *my students begged me to let her stay in the classroom because Ms. X's calling*
> *her out in front of her friends and everyone else was extremely humiliating. I*

complained to the principal; however, my concerns were ignored. Also, rather than "modifying" assignments and teaching to the students, the special education teacher would give students answers to tests/assignments and would write papers for them. This even happened on state-mandated tests. She even told me that she did this. The final straw came when I heard her tell students that they were "worthless and wouldn't amount to much." I wasn't the only frustrated regular education teacher in the school. Several others complained about the lack of professionalism, enthusiasm, and ability. However, those concerns were continually ignored by administration

Same Story, Different School

Kathleen experienced similar issues. As she wrote in 2007,

Sadly, my memory of these days is starting to fade. Although I had to make several adjustments for inclusion kids, I don't have any specific anecdotes that really stick out in my mind. I could talk some about the push to get the special ed. inclusion kids pulled from regular classes for state-wide testing so that they could take un-timed tests with limited assistance (such as mediators reading the test aloud, etc.) because we were on a NCLB target list for this specific demographic . . . but that's not anything new or exciting. Perhaps I could remember a little more about the grade adjustments that they prompted me to make (even when the kids were obviously unconcerned with their grades). What about the senior who qualified for special ed. services but his parents did not want him labeled? He was a football player who should have failed my class, but the then-principal pushed for me to let him re-test the exam with a grade adjustment on the side so that he could graduate. This brings up the question: Is it ethically wrong to provide special services to someone who has refused them when they find themselves in trouble?

Full Inclusion: It's a Nightmare

When interviewed in May 2005, Shawn expressed concern over his school's decision to implement a full inclusion model the next academic year. Although the inclusion model is the preferred model, and legal requirement, Shawn's issue was with the lack of preparation and support for students and teachers.

You should come back next year, uh, we're doing full inclusion. No special ed classes . . . I have a friend who teaches in another county that's been doing that for a few years and says it's a nightmare. He's like, "these poor kids. I have a sophomore that's on a kindergarten reading level and he's expected to do Shakespeare." Some of the teachers here . . . have special ed kids who have never been in a regular classroom, with IQs less than 50 and we have to put them in there [regular classes] next year. I don't know what's gonna happen.

Dealing with some of the levels of kids . . . like their IEPs, [they] can only have multiple choice tests, with only two questions, with only two choices . . . and seniors who miss 58 days in one semester allowed to do the make-up work. And, when the make-up work is not close enough, well is there anything else we can [do]? It's like, here's my grade book, put the grades you want for them in, and I can't believe you want their name on one of your diplomas. I'll never claim them as a student.

We Had the Opportunity

I had a kid who never came to class. His IEP said that emotionally if he needed to leave he could leave. He'd go up and take a nap in the special ed room. He came to class 12 times in the entire semester and passed cause I had to send all of his papers, all his tests, everything up to that room and I'd just get 'em back at random intervals. And when he's in class, you know he made 50s, tops. He's making 90s out of the class and I mean, I know there's some pressure off when you're taking that test but I also know that he's not getting any of the material in class and he's taking the test whenever, however, and he gets to pass. It's just frustrating that he can go to football practice every day just fine . . . remember the plays, catch the ball, and you've got a special ed teacher who's a good lady but she goes, "Well he needs an outlet for his aggression and he has one on the football field." It's like, you know, you're trying to graduate him and in two years, unless he's a forest ranger, where nobody's going to bother him and he's not gonna flip out, what have you taught him?

Cs for everybody

And we had the opportunity, when he was at school, to make him into something and that opportunity's taken away by what's supposed to be helping him. You need to do work even when you don't feel like it because that's just part of life or we're not going to advance you. If you make them do that, it's amazing what they're capable of. All these IEPs, and all this No Child Left Behind just says if they're not willing, you can't make them. And what ends up happening on the school level is pass them anyways and it's just so frustrating. In fact I got called into the principal's office one time because that kid who never came to class and said that if they made me pass him I would quit my job. And somebody told her [the principal] and I said well, "I did say it. I was frustrated." I shouldn't say stuff like that but, but that's kind of the level some of this teaching is on. It's like they don't suspend him for cussing me out in the middle of the class and throwing the book across the room. I would quit my job because I can't stand to be here anymore. And then you get that frustrated but you're like, well, that's just how it is now. Then he comes on back to class. You're like I gotta find a way to just try and do something with this [situation], but then everybody in that class knows you can act that way and every kid below them knows, hey, at this school you can do that and get away with

*it. It just gets worse and worse and worse. You've gotta get past all that. Next year
we joke about like okay, hey Cs for everybody, no real assignments, maybe we can
teach them some values just by talking about them in class, without requiring them
to do anything and then at least we did them some form of education, some service
to their life and, you know, what happens I don't know.*

Those Kids are Clueless

Although the excerpts above were from our May 2005 interview, nearly
all teachers (myself included) were very frustrated over special education
policies at our schools. I (Lisa) can remember getting notification about one
month into the school year stating that it was basically up to me to figure out
who had IEPs and who needed accommodations by going to the files in the
main office and searching through them myself. With five classes of 20–30
students each, that was a monumental task—and one I never got to before the
end of the first semester. Moreover, it was one that, as a classroom teacher,
was not my responsibility. The excerpts and figure below, also from Shawn,
came less than 60 days into the school year. And, based on the responses from
fellow novice teachers, were not isolated to him.

*I actually had a special ed teacher known here as Exceptional Education (ex-
ceptional my ass—thank you Matt Dillon)—anyway, this teacher comes up to me
one day and says—I don't know what to do—those kids are clueless. Who needs
a department for that—I could have diagnosed that. So I propose ITP's—Individual Teaching Plans. I have already met with myself and we have decided on
an appropriate plan of action. (See Figure 1.)*

Almost immediately after he included the ITP in an email to the group,
Shawn received many responses back from his fellow novice teachers.

*Your "ITP" was hilarious, Shawn. I hear you. My fundamental kids are won-
derful and sweet for the most part, but I do have lots and lots of those little
abbreviations and acronyms floating around, trying my patience and burying
me in paperwork. And of course, I just got the IEP information for most of them
today, and I suspect they will continue to trickle in . . . why wait a week to tell
me a child is 75% deaf?! And furthermore, why couldn't I tell? I thought maybe
she had a mild speech impediment . . . Erin*

*Keeping up with special education stuff. That's hilarious. I pretty much have
decided I'll never be able to do that. After 3½ weeks into the semester, the ESE
(that's sort of equivalent to special education I guess) teachers finally got all the
IEP info into our boxes. Guess what, over half the students in each of my classes
has an IEP (or whatever they call it down here.) Sorry, I don't think I'll be able*

Mister Paiva suffers from a number of teaching disorders that affect his quality of life:

O.D.D.D.—Oppositional Defiance Defiance Disorder - teacher does not respond well to those who do not respond well.

A.D.H.D.—Teacher does not have enough of an attention span to repeat instructions or assignments more than once.

O.E.D. - Oral Explosive Disorder—levels of frustration may cause vulgar comments to be addressed to students—i.e. "Shut your hole you little bastard!" or any comments that begin with "Are you F*!#ing . . . (deaf, blind, crazy, etc.)?"

Accommodations to be made:
Teacher needs as much time as he requests to complete any grading related to English.

If teacher becomes overly frustrated he must be allowed to leave the room and go to a "safe place" for no less than 15 mins and as long as necessary.

An aide must be provided to generate all tests and to take over teaching when his ADHD ODDD or OED are "acting up."

Teacher is only required to meet ½ of the national/state teaching requirements and the documentation does not have to be written—oral documentation is all that is required.

Teacher may choose which ½ of teaching requirements he will meet and cannot be fired or docked pay for not meeting half of the requirements.

Teacher must meet with problem student parents at least once a week and the parents must explain why that student is a failure every week.

If the teacher chooses, please just give him his paycheck and let him stay home for the rest of the year.

These issues will all be addressed on a yearly basis, if further accommodations are necessary - they will be made.

Figure 1.   ITP for Shawn. Originally published in Scherff, L. (2008). Disavowed: The stories of two novice teachers. *Teaching and Teacher Education*, 24, 1317–1332.

to put all 45 of my ESE students on the front row. Or make sure they can hear me when I'm yelling over students, or can see the board through the giant afro (white kids included) on the kid in front of them.

And as for attention to reading? Screw it. If they can keep their heads off the desk and at least understand the directions, then we're doing okay. I have never been in a situation where not just one, but maybe even half of the class needs me to repeat instructions 3–4 times before they are finally paying attention enough to listen. Right now, I'm over the whole thing. I won't quit or anything, what else would I do? But I'm definitely not enjoying myself right now—Dan

LISA AND MIKE'S ANALYSIS

As the stories and cases in this chapter show, special education and/or inclusion, as implemented and coordinated at each of the high schools, was not working. In fact, not one teacher offered an example of effective special education policies. Lane—as a first year teacher—taught a tenth grade class with both an autistic student and a student with Down Syndrome with little assistance from the special education department. All of my classes had both ESE and ESL students—and I (Lisa) never saw or had help from either department. In fact, I never found out exactly which students were officially labeled as ESE and/or ESL.

None of us were provided the information or tools or conditions to be the most effective teachers of special education students, or even good teachers of special education students. Not one teacher was provided with the amount of special education assistance—either through a special education teacher or the special education department. Yet, if these very same students were not provided the accommodations and modifications required by their IEPs, then we would be the ones blamed, not the special education teachers or department. As a teacher educator, how do I prepare pre-service teachers for this situation without making them want to quit before they begin?

A great deal of new teachers cite paperwork and working conditions as reasons for leaving the profession. In these cases, issues related to special education encompass both of the above mentioned issues. Teachers, and in particular new teachers, continuously express large levels of frustration related to special education. These new teachers, like many, have taken a course in special education which is not enough to prepare them for the realities of teaching in inclusive settings. Veteran teachers with years of experience in differentiating instruction also express great frustration over the decisions they have to make with special education issues.

While the issue of special education and inclusion of special needs students remains a debate among educators and policy makers, there are still things that can be done at the local school level to prepare teachers for students with special needs. First, communication is essential. New teachers must have direct communication with special education teachers, the special education department, school administrators, and parents related to the special needs students they serve. Lisa earlier expressed the requirement to search through files and review IEPs of special needs students. To a first year teacher, this can be a daunting and uncertain process. Keeping in mind that new teachers are in search of the "right way" of doing things, many issues with special education are still undecided. Also, new teachers must have support networks related to special education issues. An assigned special education teacher is not enough to make sure new teachers know what they need to know about IEPs and special education. Part of local school professional development sessions for new teachers should be dedicated to special education needs, issues, and regulations.

The new teachers in these cases face a large professional decision related to standards and expectations. In their preparation programs, prospective teachers are taught to hold high expectations for all students and to hold themselves accountable if a student does not perform. The structure of special education in many schools has yet to be defined. Without proper structure and guidance in schools, new teachers like the ones in these cases feel as if they are sacrificing high standards and expectations for their students to succumb to the legalities of special education.

Questions for Teacher Educators and Teachers

- How can teacher education programs prepare pre-service teachers for teaching special education students—especially when little to no assistance is provided by the special education department?
- Are there any existing successful models for preparing content area teachers to work with special education teachers?
- What are content area teachers' rights and responsibilities when it comes to special education students? Special education teachers? Inclusion?
- What advice would you give the teachers featured in this chapter?

Questions for Administrators

- How are new teachers to your school or system inducted into the philosophy and practices with special education students?
- What role do special education teachers play with general education teachers and is this communicated to new teachers?
- How do new teachers learn which of their students have IEPs?
- If you asked your new teachers what decisions they are forced to make related to special needs students, what would they say?
- Who is responsible for making sure new teachers understand how to read IEPs and ensure compliance?
- Who serves as the new teacher's advocate when dealing with litigious special education issues?

Chapter Ten

The Emotional and Professional Development of Teachers

Nicole, the focus of this chapter, represents the new teacher who seems to be doing okay on the surface, yet, whether due to personal, emotional, and/or pedagogical issues, is lacking the self-efficacy to do his or her best. One of the hardest things to do as a teacher is put on brave face for students and *teach* when events in one's personal life (breakups, illness, loss of a loved one, etc.) take a downward turn.

Young teachers, especially, are often torn between their work and their social lives as they make the transition from college student to "adult." This is sometimes complicated by moving far from home or where they attended college. Like any other graduate who enters the world of work, some novices have to figure out if teaching is the career for them. Nicole had two degrees and an internship, yet she was perhaps not ready for the real world of teaching.

In this chapter, we present excerpts from some of her emails, spanning from August 2004 through March 2006, to offer a glimpse into the life of a teacher who—for whatever reason(s)—did not find her niche in the profession. We do not do this sensationally, but rather we hope that by reading through her struggles it might make administrators more aware, by her words and actions, of teachers in their schools who might be going through similar struggles. Because I (Lisa) consider myself "too close" to Nicole, and her back story, I refrain from providing any analysis in this chapter.

CASE #16: LOST IN THE PROFESSION

August 2004: Jobless . . . for a few weeks

I questioned a lot of things when I was unable to get a job in the summer. I unwillingly moved back home, and then almost lost my father. My mother and

I literally spent almost two weeks in the hospital with him. I understandably thought my prayers had been answered when I heard from the principal at Rachel's school and was offered the job I now have. . . . But being dropped into three classes of freshman two weeks after school has started has NOT been anything but a nightmare. In fact, I am still squatting in Rachel's apartment. All of my things are back at home, because this all happened so fast. I am afraid I have gotten in way over my head. Some days I think that living at home and selling jewelry wouldn't have been that bad. . . . But I'm here now. So I better figure it out soon . . .

September 2004: Temporarily Broken and Bruised

Yesterday the little monsters broke me. I waited until the last student walked out the door fourth block, but just barely, before I started sobbing. I couldn't hold it in a second longer, and it felt oh-so good. I tried to clean myself up before venturing out of the room, but I was all blotchy and puffy. I didn't want anyone to know just HOW frustrated and at-my-wits-end I really was, but I received hugs from three people after just walking down the hall. Later we had a new teacher meeting, and I think it made me appreciate my school for the first time. This school may have some organizational issues, some rough students, and various other kinks to iron out. But I have honestly never seen such support. After the meeting, several teachers and two of the principals stayed late to talk to me about the problems I've been having. We must have been there for well over thirty minutes. They told me equally horrifying first-year stories, gave me advice, and made me feel welcome and appreciated. These people really care; it wasn't an act. I could see it in their eyes, and I could feel it. Though I knew that I was still going to wake up and see the same little shits in my classroom, it didn't seem so bad.

My assistant principal kept her word that she would help me out. She came by my hell-class and talked to my students for a good ten minutes about their behavior. We worked out a discipline plan for the severely discipline-challenged. And the guidance counselor personally dropped by my room to discuss the over-crowding problem in my classes. I was guaranteed that my class sizes would drop from almost 40 to around 20 each.

I can't say that I would have chosen this for myself, but I think this will be a year of growth. I left the building today feeling strong instead of weary. I didn't frown at the way my work shoes sunk into the sand (which is EVERYWHERE) or the promise of rain that was held in the clouds . . .

October 2004: Depression and Deserting

October 2

Wow. I feel like I've been sequestered from the world for weeks. I haven't checked my email or talked to any of my old friends in a month. I haven't wanted to. I haven't wanted to do a thing but come home and crawl in bed. I dread the mornings and curse my job. However, today I decided I needed to catch up on life in the "outside" world. After I read everyone's latest messages, I cried. Everything you guys said reflects how I have been feeling since I came here. It was like looking into my own soul, and somehow that made me feel better.

I know that I am not the teacher I was last year. I no longer spend hours grading papers and planning, things that I once enjoyed. I no longer view my students as the little brothers and sisters I never had. . . . I no longer miss them when we have long weekends or I go out of town . . . I once spent all of my time at school and loved it. I was on committees, helped with the yearbook, and coached. I went out to eat with other teachers every week, and even dated one. I could hardly believe that I would get paid one day to do something I loved so much . . .

Now, the thought of 1200 dollars a month hardly seems to compensate for the work I do. Like Lane, my stomach remains in a knot. I have migraines regularly, and it is not at all odd to spend hours throwing up when I get home from school. I have been in my apartment for three weeks and haven't unpacked yet. Sometimes I don't even bother curling my hair or putting on makeup in the morning, a definite sign of depression.

It's hard to be in the ethnic minority, because I don't really understand the culture my students embrace. Their values are completely foreign to me as well. Many come from broken homes or abusive homes. Some engage in prostitution; some sell drugs. . . . And most seem to live by a "just get by" mindset. Even the smallest students in my classes seem ready to argue or fight if they are approached by anyone. It was a sad day when I had to send two "mousy" girls to the office for literally beating the shit out of each other. It's all they seem to know, and that scares and saddens me.

It seems absurd that this is considered normal. I think It's appalling that the administration can't control the student body. There are serious fights at least once a week in the hallways, and it is customary for teachers to press charges against students for being shoved down or for having had something thrown at them in class. Yet, no one is alarmed. We have somewhere between 1700 and 2000 students and one policeman. I haven't seen him, but am told that he does actually do something besides sit in his office with his hand down his pants.

There are days when I actually think I hate my students. They steal things from me, they tell me off to my face, they argue when I give them simple directions. The majority of the little bastards don't want to learn, and they make it near impossible for anyone that does. They definitely make it impossible to teach. I am just there, it seems, to make sure that no one gets killed. I have no control over them AT ALL. This makes me feel like a failure as a teacher. It makes me resent them, and it makes me resent the administration.

I don't know how I will last a year here. Sometimes I don't know how I will last until December. But I don't want to be a quitter or a failure. I have a car payment and tons of bills.

October 21

Two weeks ago I had reached my breaking point. My "students" had thrown their last paper wad, tipped over their last desk during lecture, fought their last fight (in the classroom), and stolen the last thing off my cart. I could not stand the thought of the misery lasting until December. I gave them my two-week notice, and the dark storm cloud above my head lifted.

And so, I had made my decision. I was going HOME. Hallelujah! My heart was singing, but it was still hard to look at the small number of kids I've grown attached to and tell them the news. I WILL miss a few of these little faces. (I am human, after all.) BUT some will only come as dark reminders in the night of what can happen to children who grow without love and discipline. . . . My hell-raisers took my resignation as an open invitation to become EVEN WORSE than before (yes, it WAS possible). They made me so mad, I had to stifle down cuss words almost every day. I was greeted by my third block students with "Only one more week, Thank God." And each day the countdown resumed. Little bastards.

November 2004: Relief after Resignation

November 17

Three weeks ago, I walked out of my school for the last time. I considered many factors and talked to many different people before I made that decision. I have never had to work so hard to defend myself, and many of the things that were said to me still hurt. But I know that I did the right thing for ME. Ironically, the decision that I made probably saved my career. I know that I want to teach. I love literature. I love writing. I love the look that kids get on their faces when they finally get something for the first time. I love the way it feels to coach, to see the pride that a well-played tennis match can inspire. There isn't anything that I'd rather do.

But for me, watching a mob of kids run to the edge of the courtyard to participate in a fight makes me kind of sick. I shouldn't have to wonder if the student who threatened to go get her gun out of her locker as she walked out of class was serious, have to replace my school supplies every week because they keep getting stolen, or be cussed out almost every day. The paperwork is rough. The parents can be more than trying. But we had excellent training, and every job has its trivialities. (Is that even a word?) The fact was that I was starting to hate every part of my job, along with the idea of teaching in general . . . and I just don't think it has to be that way.

Last week the superintendent of our school system was fired. This week, officials asked the rest of the board members to step down. Our entire district is on probation. Violence is becoming the norm in most of the public schools, and the administration is still in denial about how serious it really is. A lot of the fingers here are pointing at the teachers, and we really need a heck of a lot more support in the classroom than we're getting. Having our teachers take the PSAT (among other asinine ideas) is NOT going to solve the problem.

I do not regret my decision. I do feel guilty sometimes, though. I really miss some of my students and co-workers. At this point in my career, however, I don't want to be a super-hero. I think the pay-off would be greater, if I could survive. . . . But what's wrong with being a regular hero at a school that fits me better? I have an interview this Friday, and I'm just hoping that they will give me another chance to teach.

November 21, 2004

I have to pack up my apartment by the end of the week, and I still have no idea where I'm going.

My interview was in B-- County, which is a delightfully small, rural county. I have been sending them resumes and application letters for over a year, and there is nothing I'd love more than to finally get a job there. I love the city, love driving in 8 lanes of traffic, love seeing the tall buildings, and love having a Pottery Barn right there in the mall. That isn't even mentioning the fact that I am getting my last paycheck in a week, gulp . . . and I do miss having a productive role in society.

I probably went on six interviews this summer. I was really getting the hang of it, too. So when this one came up, I didn't think much of it. Maybe it was just the fact that I wanted it so much. Maybe it's related to my experiences here . . . . I don't know. But I have never been so nervous before an interview. I fumbled through a few of the questions, forgot some of the things I was going to ask them, and ended up crying as soon as I got in the car to go home. It was horrible.

January 2005: Home Sweet Home?

Well, as I sit here typing on my parents' computer I try to think about last year . . . And it's hard. I was sure that I learned so much, but now I can't seem to remember why I left, or exactly what I learned . . . I miss my freedom, my space, my privacy, and my friends SO much. I adore big cities and miss the excitement. I remember when all of us went through the first months of teaching . . . It was rough. Now things seem to be falling into place for everyone, and I'm so glad. But part of me wonders if I will have to go through all of it all over again, or if I can just kind of pick up where I left off . . . Part of me feels like I am "home" every time I walk into the classroom (even though it's a different one every day). I don't feel as if I can escape it; it's where I'm supposed to be. But there's another part that's scared—I wonder if I can put up with that for twenty-five years.

I guess I'm just scared and confused. It's like falling off of a horse . . . I'm thinking about how much I love to ride but hating the horse, too. I think about some of the others who were taking a year off and wonder how they are handling things.

February 2005: Just Getting By

I am subbing at my old high school. Some days it's strange, and I feel like I am 16 again. Students' faces resemble those of friends I once knew. I know exactly what the little monkeys do when they ask to go to the restroom and come back fifteen minutes later . . . And I still can't possibly call my teachers by their first names . . . Other days, the familiar surroundings just remind me of how much I have changed in the past ten years. Gladly. The small-town politics here are beyond frustrating. I have seen ads in the paper for a Football Coach (small print warning there are also teaching duties involved), and work with a handful of those who also graduated from THS. I suspect some of them are here to relive their glory days. The kids worship them more than respect them, and I wonder how much learning goes on in their rooms . . . We all know the type. I am glad for the different experiences I have had, but long to have my own classes and my own room. I miss teaching.

I still don't know why my life has taken such crazy turns lately, but I hope that August [2005] will find me back in the English classroom. I'm trying to be positive, and I am grateful for the things I'm learning. But I'm a little bummed out, and I am lonely here. I'm ready to get back on the horse. (and gallop out of this city!!!)

March 2005: "I'm Out of the Loop"

I admit that I don't read my email as often as I should and even less often actually reply. I think sometimes it's a little awkward for me to read all of your emails. I don't have a lot to say, mostly due to my present work situation . . . and I think this makes me a little sad sometimes. I'm out of the loop right now. I miss having a classroom, and a permanent group of kids, and even grading papers and complaining about asinine parents. When you spend so many years trying to figure out what it is that you were put here to do with yourself, and then something prevents you from doing it, it can be frustrating and disappointing.

If there is one thing that I can say about the past four months, it has DEFI-NITELY been a learning experience. I'm ready to send out my applications this week and start all over again. I feel like all of the experiences I've had have better prepared me for whatever the future has in store this time. I have actually subbed in grades 5–12, and I spent an entire month teaching fifth grade. Fifth graders are a different animal, and elementary school is an entirely different world! I'm so glad I got that opportunity, but you can just see me sitting on the floor in a circle reading aloud to 10-year-olds . . . It was hilarious. (I ditched the skirts and heels after a week!) I taught a unit on fractions (that was a challenge) and reviewed for the Terra Nova exams. I just couldn't get used to lining them up to go to lunch, having bathroom breaks, and then there's free time . . . They definitely don't take home as many papers to grade or spend as long planning,

but I love high school. And teaching math? I shouldn't be teaching ANYONE
math!! I have a hard enough time figuring out the tip at the bar . . . :)
I miss you guys! You are doing so well, and your first year is almost over!!!

October 2005: New Year, New Job . . .
Oh My God, what am I doing?

October 2

I am finally at a school where the children want to learn. They are polite; they
are intelligent, and they do their work. It is a dream compared to the halls of my
other high school. But I am dealing with a whole new set of political issues, which
I discovered the first week of pre-planning. Our principal actually told us that it
was sometimes better to appease the parents than to "make a fuss" over a few
points when grading. I was introduced to the "recovery policy" of our county,
which enables any child who is unhappy with his/her grade to do extra work to
pull up their overall average. I was told I could not move a student for excessive
talking, because she might tell her parents I was "picking on her," and that might
"take me somewhere I wasn't ready to go." As the weeks passed, I found that some
of the women in my department are more than willing to do catty, unethical, and
childish things in order to get ahead . . . or put others down. I found that nobody
could be trusted, including people I had considered "friends."

It seems as if what I do is never enough. I'm working 60 hours a week and
more . . . and barely making ends meet. The students are learning; they are do-
ing well, and I adore them. I'm living for those poems, smiles, notes, and visits
from my students. I see a handful of them embracing literature and writing, and
it makes me feel alive. But should I feel guilty for wanting a house someday, for
wanting a wedding, for wanting to pay off my student loans?

October 31

I feel like I am having a nervous breakdown, or perhaps some type of quarter-
life crisis. I have really started to hate my job. I hate what I have to do when I
am not in class, the political bullshit that I put up with, the snotty attitude of the
kids, their absolute whininess and laziness, the arrogance of the other teachers
. . . women who are all just doing this job "for fun," to take up time . . . I could
just go on and on and on forever.

I don't think I can just be happy with existing in this mediocrity forever. I
wanted to do something great with my life, and I feel that I am baby-sitting.
I feel trapped. I want to break out of the room, run down the hall and head
straight for my car. I thought I was feeling better about everything, but after
13 people in a row asked me if they could go to the bathroom, I was forced
to ask myself what the HELL I was doing with my life. . . . Being a bathroom
monitor? How boring! I don't feel challenged. I don't feel stimulated. I don't

feel that I am making any sort of difference. I don't know if I can do this. I don't want to do this. Yet, I don't see a way out in the near future.

Is it me? Am I going to be happy doing anything? Do I even have a real "place" in the world, or is everything relevant? I wanted to put in at LEAST another year before I re-evaluated the situation, but I have such little desire to do this for another year. Maybe it wasn't the violence? Maybe some of it was actually teaching itself. I only have one question . . . Why were things so different when I was an intern?

January 2006: Another one of us leaves teaching?

It's been awhile since we've all talked. How many of you are still plugging along? How many of you have gone on to explore bigger and better things than teaching? I am, I suppose, about to be included in the latter group. Part of me has seen this day coming for a long time, but the idealistic part of me has refused to let go. Now I have reached a figurative fork in the road, and cannot turn back. But perhaps I can, at least, be happy now. I went to work today for the sole purpose of entering in my grades and getting the hell out of there. It was supposed to be a holiday, but was later changed to a work day for various reasons.

Anyway, it's no secret that some of us have been struggling on and off this whole school year. I definitely have been. But I try not to let my coworkers know this. I thought that coming to work, staying late, and trying to do the best that I could might suffice. I spend twelve hours here some days, and have basically no social life anymore. I work for a school, and in a county, that considers itself the BEST. Today, I was basically told that I don't fit the image. I am not happy enough; I don't coddle the students enough; and apparently despite my sponsoring Freshman Council and coaching tennis, don't do enough. The whole time I know she wants to add that I don't fit in with the rest of my department. I was told that she didn't know if she could "see me here again next year," and was told that I needed to have a meeting with her to figure out what I was going to do and discuss a few other issues that have arisen. It just pisses me off. But perhaps this is God's way of guiding me to wherever it is that I am supposed to be. Because I have known since around November that it probably wasn't teaching, but couldn't get up the courage to admit it to myself. It's sad when you realize that one of your dreams or goals has missed the mark. It's embarrassing to think that it's so obvious that everyone else can tell. But so many of us have been through this process, that at least I know it isn't just me. I have heard of Rachel, Toni, and Shawn pursuing other things and finding happiness. Now I can do the same. I'd like to know how your years are going, and especially for those of you who expressed discontent earlier . . . if you have advice or stories, please share them.

March 2006: Teaching is a Very Small Part of this Job

I was simply too idealistic going into this profession. I see the interns here--all starry-eyed and excited about "making a difference" in the world. I was like that once. I think we all were. I wanted to teach because I sincerely love to write. I am fascinated with the different forms of writing and hoped that I could somehow transmit this to others. I wanted to find the budding writers and nurture them. I wanted to find the readers and help them to get more out of their reading. I really did believe that I could make a difference. Nothing else really mattered.

But it seems to me that idealism is not a tool that is valued or nurtured in this field.

Teaching is a very small part of this job. The bulk of it is politics. There are so many unwritten and unspoken requirements. They don't care if you love your job, love the kids, or have a shred of talent. You only have to keep the parents happy, fill out your paperwork, make sure your averages are "where they should be" and that the kids standardized test scores are high enough, that you sponsor enough activities to prove you are involved, that you get along with your department members, and that your lessons look like everyone else's. There are so many guidelines as to what you can and cannot teach, so much documentation and CYA paperwork to do that it becomes impossible to actually just teach.

My administration tells us to let any child who is failing do extra work. They tell us to accept late work because "It matters if the child grasps the concept, not when he/she turns the work in." This isn't what I signed up for. They aren't learning a damn thing, but how to use politics and money to get what they want. And if I do try to teach them anything about responsibility or life, I am rewarded with a horrified email or meeting.

It's like a fog and lights show. It seems to be very impressive, but it's nothing special. As long as the audience is happy, it's considered a success. But how much fun is it when they tell you how much fog to produce and limit the number of lights you can have? To me it is drudgery. I work long hours. I make an unimpressive salary. And there is no respect. I cannot even do what I actually wanted to do--make a difference.

I am working the last 40-something days left of this year. I am trying to find another job . . . One that will earn me respect and help pay my loans . . . I may not make a huge difference, but I think I will be a hell of a lot happier. . . .

MIKE'S RESPONSE

Nicole has much to offer school administrators. While teacher preparation programs work to make sure that students entering teacher preparation programs arc suited to teach, they cannot always identify which ones will and will not succeed. Nicole appears to have a great passion for teaching, in particular her subject area. It is seemingly evident from the emails from Nicole that she is struggling with the realities of the classroom. While the realities of teaching often provide the greatest shock for new teachers, they appear to have a greater impact on Nicole.

One of the first observations from Nicole's case is the need for transition into the profession from her university program. In many other professions, the transition into the actual job is more incremental and not as abrupt. While teacher candidates do have usually the equivalent of a semester long internship (or in Nicole's case a full year), they are then essentially thwarted into the profession and are held to much the same standards as those who have been in the profession for years. School leaders place a lot of focus induction and mentoring, but there are so many personal issues one faces as he or she is entering the profession. Nicole appears to struggle with many of the personal aspects of entering this profession.

As a result of her experiences, Nicole appears to conclude that she was not meant for the classroom. School leaders are placed in tough situations when they encounter a teacher such as Nicole. She was formally prepared for teaching and has made a professional commitment to the field. However, upon entering the profession, she struggles. While it is not uncommon for many new teachers to second guess their career choices, Nicole is different. She pursues different teaching assignments hoping that each experience will be different, yet she concludes that teaching is not for her. School administrators often have to engage in these tough conversations with such teachers in an effort to guide them. School leaders have to recognize when induction, mentoring, and other such support mechanisms are not productive for new teachers. New teachers like Nicole must know that it is okay to make the decision to exit the profession; unfortunately, school leaders have to assist in allowing new teachers to realize this.

Nicole offers another important aspect for all new teachers. She clearly holds an aversion to the resistance she receives to her idealism. Like many new teachers, Nicole enters the profession with ambitions to teach children her subject matter--English. She is clearly passionate about the role of the teacher and the subject. While she is experiencing difficulty in her new role as a teacher, one of the frustrations she voices is the way in which her idealistic views appear to not be accepted. School leaders, in an attempt to prepare new teachers for the classroom, sometimes require that new teachers rid themselves of this idealism. While teachers do have to grasp the realities of the classroom in order to succeed in the profession, keeping the idealism they have in their early career can be the factor that allows them to become truly great teachers.

Questions for Administrators

School leaders will encounter a new teacher like Nicole in their careers.

- How can school leaders recognize the difference between teachers who are in the wrong profession from those who need additional induction and support?

- What are the observational factors that school leaders should be aware of to alert them to a teacher who is struggling like Nicole?
- Is it the school leader's role to assist Nicole make a decision to exit teaching?
- How might school leaders engage in critical conversations with individuals to help them determine their career choice?

Nicole also possesses a strong passion for teaching and her subject, yet she concludes she was not meant for teaching.

- How can school leaders embrace the idealism that new teachers have when they enter the profession and use it their advantage?
- In our attempts to prepare new teachers for the realities of the classroom, how can we be sure to not require that they absolve themselves of the idealism that can allow them to become exemplary teachers?

Chapter Eleven

Piling on the Paperwork and Pushing Teachers Out

I think we are all probably choking on the paperwork at this point! One of my biggest problems is that lesson plans through August 20 are due this Friday yet I can't get my computer to work to log me on the grade book program—August 10, 2004

The paperwork never ends!!!! We are expected to turn in detailed lesson plans every Friday . . . I have spent hours documenting things I could have just entered into the MANDATORY system. My students have no attendance records because they don't seem to want to hook me up. So . . . I will have to make a trade between lesson plans and the computer system!—August 23, 2004

My gradebook program STILL does not work, despite two handwritten notes and six, no count that seven, emails to our tech guy . . . Despite this, I am supposed to be "keeping accurate records" and maintaining averages for every student. I am also supposed to call at least three parents every week and document it. I have to do a "new teacher" portfolio, even though I did one in FL the first year I taught. Neither my dept head, "mentor," and "buddy" have stopped by my room once. Thank God I have not needed any of them I am truly at a loss. If it stays like this, I don't know if I can go a whole year —August 27, 2004.

The three emails above, written only days and weeks apart from one of the new teachers illustrate the frustration over the amount of paperwork and recordkeeping that is required of him or her (Scherff & Kaplan, 2006). More importantly, it shows the lack of support in place to assist the teacher in doing his or her job as expected. However, the teacher above was not a first-year novice teacher; that teacher was me (Lisa). And, I went into a "new" position with six years' experience as a high school English and reading teacher and a doctorate in education.

The cases in this chapter shed some light about the amount of paperwork, bureaucracy, and other issues to overwhelm new teachers. As Mike and I both know, there are official documents that need to be filled out (IEPs, discipline referrals, etc.), lesson plans to be written, and grades to be turned in. But, it seems that when it comes to an overabundance of paperwork, across five states the novice teachers' stories are eerily similar. We offer a few email excerpts, rather than fully developed cases to show how the same issues kept emerging.

CASE #17: NO TIME FOR TEACHING

Susan: "When do we teach?"

Talking paperwork???? When do we teach????? I mean, N-- High is the bomb when it comes to having everything computerized and being current on the latest technology---BUT my GOODNESS!!!! When did we become accountants? I mean, I'm in meetings and training every day!! We have 21 English teachers and nearly 3000 students!! We do instructional planning together, which is great!! The only downfall is that you must teach the same stuff that the other teachers teach—even the same activities!!! Nonetheless. . . . I've been busy!!! School starts at 7:20–2:00. I get to work at 6:30 and leave around 5:30 . . . no life for me—at least for now!!

Dan: I can't be a teacher if the system won't let me breathe

It wasn't my intention to paint a bleak picture of where I am, because where I am is not quite so bleak. The problem with here is not my students. They are wonderful in their own ways. They certainly do show more attitude than the kids I had in K--, but then, I had a bunch of middle-class Caucasian country students who barely even knew what an African-American or a Hispanic-American would look like and they all had church going parents who view southern hospitality as the true way to get to heaven. So certainly, they might show a little less attitude and a little more cooperation. No, the trouble with here is not my students, it's not really even the administration at my school (although there's always room for improvement there) it's more the county administration and the state of Florida itself. The very idea that I have to write up an AIP for any of my really smart students simply because they failed a test by one point in the ninth grade that they aren't even supposed to be ready for until the 10th grade is ridiculous. The very fact that many of my students who have displayed aptitude in reading and writing and simply just having a brain and using it in my English class have shown a difficulty in passing the FCAT leads me to believe that the damn test is just too damn hard. I can understand how some of my challenged students might have difficulty, but I am talking about students who are good at both. I don't know, because I haven't administered the test, and we're not allowed to look at the tests or even past examples, but I have my own suspicions that if the tests are timed, then they just aren't giving the kids enough time to finish.

Am I the greatest teacher in the world? Absolutely not!! But does that mean I need all this extra stuff they give us, I'm sorry, I meant, PILE on us? No. Last week I stayed after school at least an hour almost every day for some random meeting or other that had little to really do with me except that my job required me to be there. I can't be a teacher if the system won't let me breathe enough to actually teach. It's not as if these meetings were extracurricular activities that I chose to do, no they were New Teacher this and Faculty that, and New teacher this, and Personal Development Plan That, and AIP's and IEP's and on and on and on and on.

Kathleen: I just can't get everything done

I haven't read through everyone's emails yet (I had 55 messages waiting for me), but I was wondering if anyone else thinks that they are spending too much time on paperwork right now. Not just paperwork, but planning, grading, running copies, etc. I get to school around 7:45 and don't leave until around 4:45 or later. I just can't get everything done. My planning period seems more like a breather than anything super-productive. However, maybe this is all a combination of the first week of school craziness and the brutal catch-up I have inflicted upon myself. I am just ready to have a normal schedule again. Almost lunch, so I'm going to run (I still try to eat with my colleagues even though it is right in the middle of my planning period).

Toni: I'm all about conserving TIME, since I have none

It's like, even when I do have a "free" (I won't really call it free.) moment, my head is spinning, I'm nearly asleep, I'm busy, and just plain brain dead all at once. My grading program is finally working on my computer w/o locking it up, but i sure as hell don't plan on trusting it, so i guess it's the old calculator and gradebook method until they get it all straightened out, which they've had plenty of time to do of course. But, I'm definitely not complaining. Does anyone have any other time saving tips for grading, grading essays, keeping up with paperwork & e-mails, contacting parents who think their child is a hard-working genius, attending meetings or getting to work? I mean, maybe i could figure out a way to put in a shower & bed in my classroom, maybe a little kitchen nook. Not that i want to live there, but i'm all about conserving TIME, since i have none.

Lane: by the time I get to the kids, all of my creative efforts are spent

I don't know what exactly it is . . . I know that we are not alone as a group of former interns though. The other first-year teachers at my school are drowning in the same boat as I am, except worse because they are from out-of-state and are unfamiliar with all that wonderful paperwork that thankfully was indoctrinated into our souls last year.

As far as where we are teaching goes, I am at one of the nicest schools in one of the best counties. The faculty is great—but the parents are horrid. I honestly talk to the parents just as often as I do the kids. If I am not in front of my students, I am emailing some nosy parent who wants to know if their child turned in their homework that day. We also have a strict curriculum that we must follow each nine weeks, with a specific list of skills requiring mastery by the end of the nine weeks, gauged by a PBA (performance-based assessment). Oh yeah, did I mention that they read two novels every nine weeks?

I think my pissiness is directed to NCLB. My district is only obeying the policies set up by the nat'l gov't. I just wish I could teach what I want, when I want. The days when I throw out the lesson plan and teach what I want are the best days in my classes where the kids seem engaged and excited to be there. M--- is down the road at our sister school that just opened two years ago, and he told me that he threw out the curriculum a long time ago and is doing what he wants. I wish I could do that, but everyone in my dept. plans together and I have to submit my plans every nine weeks. I think the biggest thing for me is that I always feel watched. I'm constantly having to explain myself to parents and county people and whoever, and I spend most of my energy doing that instead of teaching . . . by the time I get to the kids, all of my creative efforts are spent.

Rachel: CAN I JUST TEACH???

I'm getting sick of beauracratic (sp?) bullshit. I was just informed that at the end of each semester we have to fill out a form on each student with comments on how the did on each standard! There are like 30 some odd standards! What the crap. CAN I JUST TEACH??? That would be great, thanks.

1. *Meetings: We have staff dev. meetings every Monday; one Tuesday a month we have a meeting until 5:30 (we get out at 2:30); Wednesday we have mentor/mentee meetings; Thursday I have poetry club. And on average, once a week our planning period is taken up by a meeting. They tell us to offer more tutorial time, but how am I supposed to do that when I have meetings every day after school. I don't know how many times I've had to cancel tutorial bc [because] of some mandatory meeting. Isn't it defying the purpose?*
2. *NCLB: Just let me teach what I want to teach. I am so sick of performance standards, QCCs, standardized tests.*
3. *Paperwork: Every Friday we have to turn in detailed lesson plans for the next week. Every time a kid sneezes the wrong way we have to fill out these SSP forms (student success plans) which take some time. THE PSAT. All teachers at my school have to take the PSAT. Don't ask.*

LISA AND MIKE'S ANALYSIS

As reported earlier (Scherff & Kaplan, 2006), I didn't necessarily believe student teachers' and teachers' complaints about the massive amounts of paperwork that seemed to emerge after NCLB. That is, I didn't believe them until I went back to the classroom in 2004. I literally had zero time and energy left for planning and teaching after completing all of the paperwork that was required of me. My experience mirrored that of most of the novice teachers we include in this book.

In preparing the novices for the work of high school teaching, teacher education programs cover handling the paper load, short-and long-term planning to reduce the stress of last-minute lesson plans, how classroom procedures and a "less is more" approach could cut down on their daily paper load, and when and how to use effectively use quizzes, tests, and projects in order to maximize time. Yet, somehow, we don't always prepare them for the paperwork required with NCLB. As several of the teachers asked, couldn't they just teach?

These new teachers convey very real scenarios of almost every new teacher entering the profession. In many ways, these issues are also representative of veteran teachers' concerns. The demands of paperwork and documentation are not new to the classroom; however, it seems to have become exacerbated by the requirements of NCLB. We tend to place the same demands and expectations on novice teachers as we do all other teachers who have had time and experience to prepare and adjust to the burden. As school leaders, our response is often the approach that "these are requirements" and that they are "out of our control." While oftentimes the required documentation may be out of our control, it is still important to recognize the difficulty this places especially on a new teacher who is still getting acquainted with the profession and its challenges.

In many cases, as evidenced by these new teachers, the paperwork comes from multiple sources, be it lesson plans mandated from department heads, individual teaching plans mandated from the principal, objectives mandated by a central office, IEPs required by the special education department, or student lunch numbers mandated by the cafeteria staff. The new teachers in these cases appear to be very capable individuals who are forced to make decisions about what to prioritize in regards required documentation. Keep in mind that the focus of the new teacher is the success in the classroom with students, so any requirement beyond that is often going to be perceived as a conflict with his or her teaching. School leaders might assist new teachers in this area by conducting an audit in their schools to identify all required paperwork and documentation required of new teachers. It may be beneficial to prepare new teachers in the early stages of their induction to these various requirements so that they will not be surprised as the year progresses. It may also serve to integrate the various requirements into the induction and mentoring process so that new teachers have planned and immediate assistance with the numerous requirements that come up each year.

These cases do not extract one single source of pressure for new teachers. In fact, it appears to be to the compilation of numerous small, yet important, items that serve as the obstacle for the beginning teachers. For example, the issues of getting computer support personnel to provide the necessary logins so that teachers can use the required grade book program. This is a small and seemingly easy item to fix, yet it was not done for one teacher. Nonetheless, that teacher might be held accountable for not having entered students' grades. Often in a school, once an administrator finds out about a problem such as this an order is placed for computer support and then he or she moves on to the next issue. Especially in the case of a new teacher, the school leader can provide additional support by following up on the request to make sure it is done. While this is ostensibly insignificant, to the new teacher it sends a strong message of support and eases much of the tension he or she may feel.

Another issue present in these cases is extra-curricular assignments assigned to new teachers. The teachers we featured express the need to focus on teaching, yet they get derailed by paperwork, meetings, sponsoring clubs, parent conferences, etc. While such tasks are inevitable in our profession, new teachers must have time to ease into these non-teaching aspects of the job. Some systems do not allow new teachers to sponsor or coach any sports or clubs their first semester or year in order to enable new teachers the time to focus on the demands of teaching. There is merit in this idea.

The teachers in this chapter are overwhelmed with the numerous unforeseen demands of teaching that seemingly prevent them from the focus in the classroom. For many, these are the realities that often do force good teachers to leave the profession. As school leaders, we can examine the requirements and assist new teachers by providing the support necessary—even if it means letting a student club go defunct for one year. We can also aid by preparing them for these demands in the school induction process so that they are prepared for what they will encounter. Lastly, we can support new teachers by assisting with the prioritization of the numerous demands they will face.

Questions for Teacher Educators and Teachers

• What can teacher education programs do, if anything, to prepare candidates for the non-grading paperwork load they will face?

- Should teacher educators spend class time going through and filling out examples of paperwork that their graduates will face?
- What about the non-curricular aspects of the job? Should veteran teachers only sponsor clubs and coach sports?

Questions for Administrators

- The new teachers in these cases meet the time demands of teaching with resistance as the demands take their focus away from teaching in the classroom.
- As school leaders, what can we do to assist a new teacher with prioritization of the numerous demands?
- How can we audit the various sources of paperwork and assist them in preparation?
- How can mentors be useful in aiding a new teacher with all of these unforeseen issues?
- Is it effective to limit the amount of extra-curricular activities a new teacher can sponsor or coach so that he or she can focus on the classroom?
- How can we be sure we are providing support in these small areas that appear to serve as a source of frustration for new teachers?
- How can we utilize technology to obtain the information necessary without requiring teachers to do reports?
- What can school leaders do to prepare parents for the way and times email will be used by teachers?

Chapter Twelve

"Superteacher"

How many times during our careers have we acted like we knew more than we did? Or we were asked to do things beyond our capabilities? Novice teachers are often asked to coach a sport or sponsor a club (sometimes those with which they have no background) in order to secure a job. However, what happens when beginning teachers are saddled with curricular responsibilities beyond their means based on initial, and sometimes faulty, thinking?

This is what happens to Jennifer, the teacher featured in this chapter, very quickly into the school year. The email exchanges that follow, chronicle the discussion among her, Dan (a fellow novice teacher), and myself between August 12 and August 14, 2004. Note that this discussion occurs less than two weeks into the school year.

CASE #18: PRESSURE TO BE A STAR

From: Jennifer

Since you guys are so supportive and whatnot, could I get a vote of confidence? I'm feeling really stressed right now because the principals at this school think I'm the "shiznit." They fell in love with the [electronic] portfolio and think that I am super-special because of it (They had never seen one before). Every day I have to hear, "Hey, that's Mrs. O - we snatched her up before Reynolds did. They sure are mad!" (Reynold's being the supreme school in the county). I feel that I have to do something awesome everyday and it is really wearing me down. I know this seems crazy to whine about—I certainly don't think I'm worth this praise. I'm a first year teacher for some Deity's-sake. What can I do?
Frazzled-First Year,
Jennifer

From: Jennifer

I know it is insane to whine about, but I don't like a lot of attention. I have become the sponsor of the Girls Service Club, band, and the school computer lab. (I know very little about computers). It is hard to get assistance from the administration with discipline because they say I'm "resourceful." I guess what I really meant to say is how do I politely point out that I can't be super-teacher? I don't want to admit a weakness and have them think I actually am not what they wanted. I think I'm fairly decent at teaching. Plus all the attention and the administration's comments have ostracized me from all of the veteran teachers. I ask the other teachers for advice and they turn around and say they should be asking me for advice. I'm getting frustrated because I'm actually inexperienced and don't know all the answers they assume I know.

From: Dan

I don't want to be a discourager, but maybe you should start by not taking so much on at once. You may have supreme organization skills, but Jeez, sponsoring three programs, settling into a new school system, and learning how to do THEIR paperwork, that's a pretty big plate for starting out. Second of all, you don't have to be a super-teacher every day, and don't let anyone make you feel like you have to. If you don't like the attention, don't stress yourself out trying to live up to it. If there's one thing I've figured out about teaching, it's that the new teachers are just as new to the faculty, as the faculty is to the new teachers. What they wanted was a young teacher with fresh ideas and a motivated spirit. They got that with you, but that does not by any stretch of the imagination, mean that you HAVE TO BE highly motivated and super creative every day. Even "super" teachers aren't "super" every day. I'm not recommending complacency, just don't be so hard on yourself, and don't let "them" grind you down. Finally, you may just have to tell them directly that you do need help. There has to be someone in that place that would be willing to share and bounce ideas off of you. Hang in there, you'll figure it out.

From: Lisa

Jennifer,
Your situation is a tough one, but one that is not your fault! Also, it is similar to what some of you experienced as interns (remember jealous and/or hostile teachers?).
Remember: your administration set this up. No, it is not right that the faculty say things like that to you. I do know a little about this. I am experiencing some of this at my school. Any time a teacher makes a comment about "something" that I seem to know a lot about, I say something like, "I was very lucky that someone gave this to me a while back" or "I don't know if I know that much; I had a fellow teacher give me _____."

You can try that, or you can do nothing and let it blow over (in other words, hide out for a while). If you know someone that will LISTEN (hint, hint: administration) tell him or her that you have had too much responsibility thrown on you. You could add that the NC curriculum is new to you and that you are only in your second year. To me, the worst thing you could do is overextend yourself. You might crash and burn (I doubt it, but you might make yourself sick and worn out in the process). I don't know if any of this has helped, but maybe it has.

From: Jennifer

Dan and Lisa,

Thanks for your comments. I feel a lot better knowing that you think it would be okay for me to say no to some things. I definitely will just have to get the gumption to do that though. I could have never anticipated having this problem. So you guys don't think it would be "weak" to go to the administration to get help? I feel that I've exhausted my capabilities with some problem boys, but they think I can still do more—detention with me after school. I spoke at length with Dr. L--- about a these problem boys, and she point blank told me not to give detention with me after school (They are drug-dealers and known to be violent). What do I do there? Ask a male teacher to stay with me? Would it be wise to say to the administration, "Hey, I'm too scared of these boys to give them detention." It sounds like I am unhappy with my school, but I actually do like it. It's just that they took my stamina for granted. Thanks for bearing with me!

LISA AND MIKE'S ANALYSIS

Jennifer faced a problem in that her administrators assumed she didn't need any help because she was proficient in the latest technology. The electronic portfolio was a requirement of her teacher education program and was intended to showcase her pedagogical skills and technological competence. Because it was such a new and novel form of technology, Jennifer's administrators falsely believed it also represented her total expertise as a teacher, forgetting that she was a first year teacher. And, this led to them assuming that she could handle a range of problems, such as discipline, on her own without their assistance. Then, she was given the responsibility for sponsoring clubs and being in charge of the computer lab—and she admits she knows nothing about computers. In essence, Jennifer was put on a pedestal and did not feel she could tell anyone that she did not know what she was doing. In her eyes, if she did ask for help, she would be letting her administrators down. That is too much pressure for a beginning teacher.

Yet, knowing Jennifer's personality and work ethic, it is not surprising that she did not say "no" to any of the responsibilities. I (Lisa) knew she was highly motivated and conscientious because I worked with her for over a year; those traits are not fully evident (or not) after an interview. Knowing teachers and their backgrounds is critical to assisting them to navigate their first years in the classroom. Had the administrators taken the time to ask her about the range of computer skills she had, they might not have put her in charge of the lab. Moreover, their comments about her "resourcefulness" put even more undue pressure on her. Worse, yet, is that their comments and actions are causing tensions between her and her colleagues. As she noted, "all the attention and the administration's comments have ostracized me from all of the veteran teachers. I ask the other teachers for advice and they turn around and say they should be asking me for advice. I'm getting frustrated because I'm actually inexperienced and don't know all the answers they assume I know."

Jennifer's case is interesting in that she represents those silent new teachers who by all appearances are doing fine. The mistake that school leaders make is that they see Jennifer and her abilities and assume she is fine, and they focus their attention and resources on new teachers who outwardly appear to having difficulty (often evidenced by classroom management issues). While Jennifer is not experiencing or expressing her areas of concern, she still needs the same caliber of support.

Jennifer represents many new teachers who feel they will be perceived as weak if they ask for help or if they say no to an extra-curricular activity. While Jennifer appears to have the ability to handle many of these responsibilities, they over burden her and prevent her from focusing on her growth as a first year teacher. The first year of teaching requires reflection on teaching strategies as well as research on what works in the context of the classroom. New teachers must have the time to focus on the learning opportunities of the first year of teaching as it sets the stage for their career. As school administrators, we too often place additional duties on competent teachers at a disproportionate rate. Since Jennifer is seemingly demonstrating competency in her first year, her school leaders assume she can manage additional duties.

Questions for Teacher Educators and Teachers

The issues between teacher education program requirements (such as the electronic portfolio) and how administrators perceive them is an issue not expected to arise for teacher educators. If anything, we sometimes face criticisms that we do not prepare teachers with enough practical experience. In Jennifer's case, her innovative practicality is what caused her problems.

- How should teacher education programs handle issues such as this?
- Do we need to articulate more clearly the purposes and rationales for requirements like portfolios? If so, who do we articulate these to?
- How can we prepare future Jennifers to say "no" and not feel ashamed in doing so?
- Is there something her fellow teachers could have done to better assist her?

Questions for Administrators

- How do the number of extra-curricular responsibilities of your new teachers compare to your veteran teachers?
- Are you often looking for new teachers to assume responsibilities that your veteran teachers are giving up?
- Does your school place any limitations on what or how many extracurricular activities a new teacher can sponsor?
- How do you evaluate a new teacher's ability to lead extra responsibilities?
- Do you afford new teachers the ability to decline a new responsibility or would this be interpreted as non-compliant?
- If asked, would your new teachers be able to come to you to convey their fatigue or frustration without being seen as weak or incompetent?
- Do you have any practices or procedures (outside of evaluation) where you meet with new teachers one on one and inquire about their individual professional concerns?
- Do you conduct exit interview or exit surveys with new teachers to identify why they leave your school or system on their own accord?

Epilogue

So, what happened to the teachers featured in this book? Well, like any story, some had better "endings" than others. Each was given the opportunity to write his or her epilogue—to reflect on their emails to the group and their time in the classroom. Some of the teachers, like Lane, are still in the profession while others, like Lisa, left more than two years ago. Every individual epilogue in this chapter is printed in its entirety, with no omissions. In some cases, however, names have been changed to protect identities.

LISA

(NOTE: The italicized portion was attached to the epilogue that Lisa sent me in April 2006)

I discovered this week that my "mentoring" teacher sabotaged me. During the past 2 years, I've gone to her with advice, and she used it against me to get me fired. Most of my students have been so sweet and want to start a protest because they think that my principal is a complete idiot. Several of the teachers have told me that they too are shocked. I'm still hurt but am moving on. My experiences at C--- [High School] and B--- [High School] have proven to me that I'm not cut out to teach high school. However, I am going to try community college next fall.

I'm leaving the teaching profession with mixed emotions. I come into education from the business world where demands and expectations are very high. For example, if a colleague didn't perform, he/she was dismissed; if a colleague was consistently absent, he/she was dismissed. Sometimes I believe that education should be run like a business: If a student is chronically absent, he/she should be reprimanded and not granted numerous opportunities to "make up" his/her work or graduate from high school. I saw this happening time and time again in my last school. A student could miss 10 or more days, never bring anything to class, never complete an assignment, and guidance office or administrative personnel look the other way and give such a student a diploma. The "real" world just doesn't work like that. People are not rewarded for incompetence!

My principal informed me that I would not be coming back next year because "I don't work well with lower-level students and the majority of our students are lower-level students." This tells me and my students that "we don't expect much from you so don't even bother trying."

KATHLEEN

I decided to become a teacher because I wanted a challenging career with opportunities to positively impact my community. I can't say that I've enjoyed every minute of teaching. In fact, after my first year I was fantasizing about moving on. I figured that when my husband and I started a family, I would reevaluate my career in teaching. Secretly, I was certain that I would be ready to quit after having a baby. After all, I couldn't continue to work this hard (particularly outside of school) or care this much when I had a child of my own to consider. Now that I find myself at this crossroads, I am amazed by how difficult the decision really is.

Teaching is a painful profession, and anyone who tells you differently has never been there. You will give up as much time and energy as any investment banker in the first few years, and yet people will not give you the respect or compensation you truly deserve. You will be asked to hold the highest standards and ethics, and yet you will be forced to compromise your philosophy of teaching based on the real life demands of your school system. You will put your heart and soul into your classes, and yet you will have your feelings occasionally, if not frequently, trampled. So do I like teaching? Would I do this again? Will I ever go back? The answer is (surprisingly) *Yes*!

I don't know if anyone ever truly understands what they are getting into when they begin a career in teaching. I certainly didn't. However, I chose this career because I wanted challenges and the chance to do something important. It is guaranteed that teachers will lose sight of their contributions under the chaos of the daily grind. There will be more opportunities to question your decision to teach than not. Still, I can stand back every once in a while and recognize that my presence in the classroom truly matters. It's not easy, but I didn't choose this profession because I wanted to do something easy.

SUSAN

Teaching is a "chosen" profession. People choose teaching as a career, not because of the great pay, but because there is a great desire to make a difference in tomorrow's America. As teachers, we dream of the perfect classroom in which all students generally desire to learn. This is not so! In fact, the classroom consists of students who only come to school because they have to. If given a choice, many would prefer to stay home. A small percentage of our students are replicas of ourselves; they want to make a difference in America. They aspire to be the next generation of America's doctors, lawyers, engineers, politicians, and teachers. Why is the percentage of motivated students so low? Why is the American schooling institution failing? Blame is shifted to the teachers—those who desire to teach, and not the learners—those unwilling to learn.

The following was sent to me from a co-worker via e-mail.

This was in the Vent section of the Gwinnett section of today's Atlanta Journal Constitution . . . pretty amazing. Can you teachers out there feel the love??

"Teachers should be held responsible for ill-behaved children. They spend the most time with these kids, know their friends, who they hang out with and actually hold them accountable for not doing their work. A failing, misbehaved child is the teacher's fault. Busy parents don't have time for these matters and they pay taxes."

Teachers are underappreciated, yet we are expected to perform miracles in the classroom with students that have been giving free will and free reign to do as they please without major consequences. Twenty years ago, high school students went to school knowing that school was for learning, it was a safe place to go to attain the "key" to their future. Ten years ago, students went to school believing that, if they wanted it, education was there for the taking—their choice! Today, students come to school unwillingly. They come because their parents make them come; they can't stay home; they come to eat breakfast; they come to socialize; they come to have fun, and if by any chance they "happen" to learn something new, GREAT! When they come to school they bring attitudes, problems, drugs, and weapons. School is no longer a safe learning environment. School has become a "stressed" learning environment.

Teachers are stressed due to increased workloads, restricted curriculum, and tolerance of disrespectful students. America's teachers are expected to be teachers, mediators, disciplinarians, doctors, counselors, parents, negotiators, administrators, custodial workers, secretaries, entertainers, problem solvers, encouragers, mentors, detectives, and teachers once again – all in a standard 60 minute class, while being governed.

Our hands are tied. We are expected to teach with our hands tied behind our backs, blinders over our eyes, and muzzles over our mouths. We are governed in our work load, our curriculum, and in the amount of tolerance from students' disrespect – yet, teachers are still expected to teach in school systems run by a majority of disrespectful and unmotivated students.

I commend those who stay in the profession despite being bound, restricted, gagged, and tied. School systems depend on us and America trusts us with the lives of those who will continue to construct America, so why not take the autonomy from the students and once again, trust teachers with the autonomy of the classrooms? When will we be allowed to teach!

NICOLE

When I think about the things that have happened over the past three years, I feel an odd mix of emotions. The first is undeniable nostalgia. I remember how much I loved teaching once, despite the fact that I was working without pay. I really don't altogether understand how, when, where, or why that started to change. . . . But it makes me sad to realize that it has.

Maybe it is all about finding the right school. I would like to think that I might still drive to work with a smile, singing along with the radio and looking forward to the day ahead if I were in that small rural school. But the truth is that I'll never know. I no longer have the desire to teach. I see critical problems within education. I see the parents and students who work the system; I see the administrators who allow this, and I recognize the flaws within this system. I no longer can say what it is that the students are actually learning. I'm not sure what it is that we're measuring. I think it's wrong that teachers work such long hours for such little pay. But the real crime is that they are often treated with disrespect by those who should appreciate them the most. They are also expected to have impeccable values, but are required at times to do things that blatantly go against them.

These problems are ones that will have to be addressed at some point. But I, for one, cannot just bide my time until this happens. God bless those of you who can.

LANE

In looking back on the past four years, I see a dramatic change in who I am as a teacher and as a human being. I think it is safe to say that the sole cause of this change would be my students.

I was thrown into, no I chose, a district and a school that thrives on unrealistic expectations and finger-pointing. Naturally, after leaving an extremely supportive community in graduate school and in my internship, this jolt shook my values and motivations to the core. When faced with adversity and opposition, I chose to complain and focus on the causes of the problem – the central office, my administrators, and accusatory parents.

The one place I chose not to explore was my own classroom. I took those frustrations into my lessons and resented my students for the actions of others. What I should have been doing was looking to my students for the solution.

I've realized that to find success as an educator requires one to focus solely on the well being of his or her students, not the external forces that are beyond anyone's control anyway. Since then, I arrive at work looking forward to teaching, not my job. I look forward to interacting with my students, seeing them grow into lifelong thinkers and questioners. This is the only way I can survive here. If I choose to dwell on the negative aspects of this profession – the ridiculous level of accountability, the endless paperwork, the blameless parents, and the puzzling hypocrisy – I would lose my mind. To be an educator, someone who teaches, not just plans lessons and handouts, I must invest what creative energy I have into my students.

To my dismay, once I began developing relationships with each of my students, I saw their desire to learn increase, which in turn motivated me to challenge myself to become a more skilled, knowledgeable teacher. The system has its flaws, that's for sure. But I am the only person who can allow those flaws to affect my quality of life, at work or at home. Instead of focusing on what decisions are being made in the front office, I should turn my eyes to the senior who still visits me every day because I am his motivation to graduate. I should keep working with the troubled junior who for the first time believes that he might go to college. I should reach out to the young girl who recently lost her mother and desperately wants comfort. I should laugh with the kid in my 8th period who makes it his goal to brighten my tired eyes after a day of teaching.

These are the reasons I am still here. I am a teacher, and I am proud to say to myself once again that I can actually do this.

ERIN

Four years have passed and I barely recognize the nervous little intern that I used to be. I tell myself my idealism is still intact, but I know it isn't. I tell myself that I will still be doing this in five years, but I'm not sure about that either. My circumstances have changed so much that I haven't been able to apply much of what I learned during the first two years, other than the necessary capacity for compassion and patience.

I went from middle-class rural and suburban schools in East Tennessee to an alternative school in metro Atlanta that serves students who have been expelled from traditional schools. Every day is a challenge, but the rewards still outweigh the difficulties. The small class sizes offer me a chance to get to know my kids better than I ever did in a traditional school, and even though my colleagues are quick to remind me that "we can't save 'em all," there is a general atmosphere of optimism most of the time.

I kick myself pretty regularly for not keeping a journal throughout this process. My own story isn't particularly titillating, but there are so many students whose stories need to be told. Isolating one for this epilogue—handing you a snapshot and saying, "here, this kid is the reason I'm still a teacher"—would be an exercise in futility. But every day one of them says or does something to remind me why I'm still here.

SHAWN

December 18, 2007

This is a fitting date to write the epilogue of my teaching career. This is my one-year anniversary of being a police officer. I think that my personal feelings about teaching are best summed up by what I have been telling my friends and family for the last year: "I thought I hated working; it turns out I just hated teaching." I love being a police officer and I love going to work every day—I never experienced that while I was teaching. It is not, however, the actual act of teaching that I hated. Over the last two years my wife has been working on her Master's degree in English and I have thoroughly enjoyed discussing the works and genres with her, helping her with her papers, and learning from her what she is learning from her professors. I love English and I love discussing it and helping others with it. This paradox has led me to the conclusion, or better yet, the reaffirmation of the conclusion that I already knew to be true about teaching–it is the environment that is allowed to exist in schools today that is the real problem with the education system. The majority of students do not have discipline or accountability. To reintroduce discipline and accountability back into the classrooms would change the level of education students are reaching, the quality and retention of teachers, and, I truly believe, society itself.

Every day I go to work, I see kids and young adults who do not have any concept of accountability for their actions. They are not only paying the price for it through the justice system, but they are also causing physical and/or mental harm to other people.

Whenever my coworkers and I are dealing with difficult youth who are swearing at us, robbing people, doing drugs, and trying to hurt us or others, my coworkers ask me with a laugh "You gave up summers off for this?" My reply is always the same, "It was exactly the same when I was teaching, except there was nothing we could do about it." In order for schools to return to educating youth, there are two aspects of education that must change.

Though they are both true, most people dismiss one or both of them. The first is that teaching is a profession that is vital to society, and teachers should not have to fear verbal or physical abuse, or failing a student who cannot do the work. The second aspect is that the youth of this nation spends 40 hours a week in schools. If their parents, their communities, and the media are failing in their social education, and they are required to be in an educational institution by law, that institution must be a center for discipline and accountability for actions before it is anything else. We need good teachers and good schools more than ever.

You do not have to be a police officer to know that education in America is failing. How has the general customer service been at any public place you have visited this past week? Have you ever not wanted to go to the mall or the movie theater because there might be a group of teenagers there – and teenagers are often rude, disrespectful, and sometimes dangerous? It is not because of the 30- and 40-somethings that off-duty police and armed security are all over the place. Many of today's students are scary, and good teachers are out of luck because the schools are not supporting them or the environment they need to have in order to teach. If you let a two-year-old eat whatever made him happy and kept him from complaining he would be dead before he was four, or at least incredibly unhealthy. This is how schools are operating today. Give students whatever makes them and their parents happy, and do not do anything to make them threaten a lawsuit. This is why so many students are graduating from high school who cannot read above a third grade level and who cannot perform simple math. This is why teachers are leaving the teaching profession.

The lack of discipline and accountability is not just affecting the students' intellectual abilities; it is affecting their actions inside and outside of school as well. No one is telling kids no. "No, you fail because you did not do the work." "No, you cannot come back to this school because you threatened a teacher." "No, you cannot attack another student during class with a desk." These are the types of acts that are going unchecked in today's schools and the problem is intensifying every year. There are countless examples of these situations—and worse—across the nation, but let me share two recent ones from my life.

I went to a domestic dispute three weeks ago where a 15-year-old child attacked his father. This 15-year-old was six feet, two inches tall and weighed 210 pounds. According to this young man, his friends and coaches at school had only told him how amazing he was at football and basketball and they never told him no. As a result of his athletic talent he was never disciplined at school. It turns out that after a year of being able to do whatever he wanted, when his dad told him he could not go to a party, he felt that he "should be able to do what he wanted to do." (His words). He proceeded to tell me that he wanted to go to the party, and when his dad told him no and stood in his way, he pushed him aside. He said that when his dad would not move out of his way, he pushed him down the stairs. Though this happened outside of school, it would be naïve to think that this young man's self-admitted sense of entitlement was not fueled, if not created, by his school environment.

The other example happened during school. A good friend of mine is an English teacher in a neighboring county. Last week one of her students, who has said vulgar sexual and threatening things to her in the past, threatened to kill her. She had done the unthinkable and failed him for not doing any of his work. This 16-year-old's response to this was "You f***ing skinny bitch. I'm gonna follow you home one day and beat your head in with a bat." His punishment was three weeks at alternative school. And since she is the only teacher for that grade level, she has to teach him again next semester because the county does not like to expel students.

Our schools are hurting, and they are not performing their function in society. We need good teachers, principals, and school boards. Is it too much to ask that students at least refrain from threatening teachers, attacking each other, or demanding to pass after doing poor or no work? If we start with that, perhaps students might even learn some of the subject matter. Until students are held accountable for their actions, however, teachers will continue to quit and schools will continue to graduate uneducated, undisciplined, self-entitled students who are detriments to society.

Young minds are an undeveloped resource, and a good teacher can make society a better place by shaping young minds into hardworking, respectful, intelligent young adults. Unfortunately, few teachers are given the environment they need to accomplish that task.

Everyone in education must make a stand to require excellence without excuses from students. More importantly, as a society we must not allow disrespect and violence from students and parents to shape the education process. My experiences in education have left me with much sympathy for teachers, a longing for what schools could be, and insight into my current clientele.

RACHEL

It's hard to believe that it's been 4 ½ years since I first stood in front of a classroom full of teenagers, lesson plan in hand, copies made, and not a clue in the world what I was about to get myself into. Now halfway into my 4th year of teaching, I feel that I'm finally beginning to find my groove. Everyone says that your first year is the hardest, and after that, it gets easier. Well I'm here to say that it does, but I continue to be challenged, frustrated, and overwhelmed every day. All of the things that I expected to feel—respected/needed/admired—don't really show up as often as I would like. When they do, however, I am reminded of why I'm here. These feelings can come from something as seemingly futile as reading a student's work and knowing that they've poured their heart into their writing, a cute note from a student, or a discussion with a student about how much they loved a book that they just read.

Some days I love my job, and I wonder why I ever took a year off or how I could ever consider leaving the profession, and some days I find myself browsing monster.com during my planning period. For the most part, I would say I'm content. I hate the perpetual paperwork, dealing with bureaucracy, parental apathy, and sometimes I think that if I hear the words "standardized testing" or "No Child Left Behind" one more time, I'll scream, but I love my students—I love hearing and reading what they have to say, them rushing to my class with a new poem they wrote or an acceptance letter from a college in hand, even how naïve they can be is somewhat endearing.

Learning to be content with my career has come from picking up on a few things along the way like realizing I don't have to be Super Teacher right off the bat, that teachers of the year have generally been doing this for ages, learning not to lose my temper in front of my students, which sometimes means stepping out into the hallway and taking a few deep breaths, or even stepping into the workroom between classes to let out a few tears and choice words. I realize I can't do this alone, so it's important for me to have a supportive group of coworkers with whom I can share and exchange ideas and an amazing group of friends with whom I can have real, "grown up" conversations and blow off a little steam.

Will I stay in this profession forever? Sometimes, I don't know if I'll even return next year. I know it takes a huge heart, tough skin, and a tremendous amount of dedication to make it as a teacher. I can only hope that my heart has the room to grow, my skin continues to toughen, and if the dedication that I feel now eventually fades, I'll have to courage to realize it and move on.

References

Alsup, J. (2006). *Teacher identity discourses: Negotiating personal and professional spaces.* Mahwah, NJ and Urbana, IL: Lawrence Erlbaum Associates and the National Council of Teachers of English.

Andrews, S. P., & Martin, E. (2003). *No teacher left behind: Mentoring and supporting novice teachers.* Paper presented at the annual meeting of the Georgia Association of Colleges for Teacher Education/Georgia Association of Teacher Educators, St. Simons Island, GA.

Ayers, W. (2001). *To teach: The journey of a teacher.* New York: Teachers College Press.

Beaudoin, M., & Taylor, M. (2004). *Creating a positive school culture: How principals and teachers can solve problems together.* Thousand Oaks, CA: Corwin Press.

Bodzin, A. M., & Park, J. C. (2000). Dialogue patterns of preservice science teachers using asynchronous computer-mediated communications on the World Wide Web. *Journal of Computers in Mathematics and Science Teaching, 19*(2), 161–194.

Boland, R. L. (1985). Phenomenology: a preferred approach to research on information systems. In E. Mumford, R. Hirschheim, G. Fitzgerald, & T. Wood-Harper (Eds.), *Research Methods in Information Systems* (pp. 439–464). Amsterdam: Elsevier.

Brock, B. L., & Grady, M. L. (2001). *From first-year to first-rate: Principals guiding beginning teachers* (2nd ed.). Thousand Oaks, CA: Corwin Press.

Brockmeier, J., & Harré, R. (1997). Narrative: Problems and promises of an alternative paradigm. *Research on Language and Social Interaction, 30*(4), 263–283.

Bullough, R. V., & Baugham, K. (1996). Narrative reasoning and teacher development: A longitudinal study. *Curriculum Inquiry, 26,* 385–415.

Cochran-Smith, C. (2004). Stayers, leavers, lovers, and dreamers: Insights about teacher retention. *Journal of Teacher Education, 55*(5), 387–392.

Connelly, F. M., & Clandinin, D. J. (1990). Stories of experience and narrative inquiry. *Educational Researcher, 19*(5), 2–14.

Connelly, F. M. & Clandinin, D. J. (Eds.). (1999). *Shaping a professional identity: Stories of educational practice.* New York: Teachers College Press.

Craig, C. J. (2003). Story constellations: A way to characterize reforming school contexts and contextualize teacher knowledge. *Curriculum and Teaching Dialogue, 5*(1), 31–41.

Creswell, J. W. (1998). *Qualitative inquiry and research design: Choosing among five traditions.* Thousand Oaks, CA: Sage.

Danielewicz, J. (2001). *Teaching selves.* Albany, NY: SUNY Press.

Darling-Hammond, L. (2003). Keeping good teachers: Why it matters, what leaders can do. *Educational Leadership, 60*(8), 6–13.

Darling-Hammond, L. (2006). *Powerful teacher education: Lessons from exemplary programs.* San Francisco: Jossey-Bass.

DeWert, M. H., Babinski, L. M., & Jones, B. D. (2003). Safe passages: Providing on-line support to beginning teachers. *Journal of Teacher Education, 54*(4), 311–320.

Estola, E. (2003). Hope as work—student teachers constructing their narrative identities. *Scandinavian Journal of Educational Research, 47*(2), 181–203.

Feiman-Nemser, S. (1983). Learning to teach. In L. Shedman & G. Sykes (Eds.), *Handbook of teaching and policy* (pp. 150–170). New York: Longman.

Feiman-Nemser, S. (1996). *Teacher mentoring: A critical review.* Washington, DC: Office of Educational Research and Improvement.

Feiman-Nemser, S., Schwille, S., Carver, C., & Yusko, B. (1999). *A conceptual review of literature on new teacher induction.* Washington, DC: National Partnership for Excellence and Accountability in Teaching.

Fibkins, W. L. (2002). *An administrator's guide to better teacher mentoring.* Lanham, MD: Scarecrow Press.

Fideler, E., & Haselkorn, D. (1999). *Learning the ropes: Urban teacher induction programs and practices in the United States.* Belmont, MA: Recruiting New Teachers.

Gold, Y. (1996). Beginning teacher support: Attrition, mentoring, and induction. In J. Sikula, T. J. Butterly, & E. Guyton (Eds.), *Handbook of research on teacher education* (2nd ed., pp. 548–594). New York: Macmillan.

Grossman, P. L., Smagorinksy, P., & Valencia, S. (1999). Appropriating tools for teaching English: A theoretical framework for research on learning to teach. *American Journal of Education, 108*(1), 1–29.

Hart, A., & Bredeson, P. (1996). *The principalship: A theory of professional learning and practice. New* York: McGraw-Hill.

Hatch, J. A. (2002). *Doing qualitative research in education settings.* Albany, NY: State University of New York Press.

Hebert, E., & Worthy, T. (2001). Does the first year of teaching have to be a bad one? A case study in success. *Teaching and Teacher Education, 17,* 897–911.

Hirsch, E. (2006, February). *Recruiting and retaining teachers in Alabama: Educators on what it will take to staff all classrooms with quality teachers.* Chapel Hill, NC: Center for Teaching Quality.

Holloway, J. H. (2001). *Who is teaching our children? Educational Leadership, 58,* 1–3.

Hough, G., Smithey, M. & Evertson, C. (2004). Using computer-mediated communication to create virtual communities of practice for intern teachers. *Journal of Technology and Teacher Education, 12*(3), 361–386.

Ingersoll, R. (2003). *Is there really a teacher shortage? A report co-sponsored by the Center for the Study of Teaching and Policy and the Center for Policy Research in Education.* Seattle: University of Washington, Center for the Study of Teaching and Policy.

Ingersoll, R. (2004). Four myths about America's teacher quality problem. In M. Smylie & D. Miretzky (Eds.), *Developing the teacher workforce: The 103rd yearbook of the National Society for the Study of Education* (pp. 1–33). Chicago: University of Chicago Press.

Ingersoll, R. M. & Smith, T. M. (2003). The wrong solution to the teacher shortage. *Educational Leadership, 60*(8), 30–33.

Ingersoll , R. M., & Smith, T. M. (2004). Do teacher induction and mentoring matter? *NASSP Bulletin, 88,* 28–40.

Johnson, S. M., Birkeland, S. E., Donaldson, M. L., Kardos, S. M., Kauffman, D., Liu, E., & Peske, H. G. (2004). *Finders and keepers: Helping new teachers survive and thrive in our schools.* San Francisco: Jossey-Bass.

Johnson, S. M., & Birkeland, S. E. (2003). Pursuing a "sense of success": New teachers explain their career decisions. *American Educational Research Journal, 40*(3), 581–617.

Kaplan, B., & Maxwell, J. A. (1994). "Qualitative research methods for evaluating computer information systems. In J. G. Anderson, C. E. Aydin, & S. J. Jay (Eds.), *Evaluating Health Care Information Systems: Methods and Applications* (pp. 45–68). Thousand Oaks, CA: Sage.

Kent, S. I. (2000). Problems of beginning teachers: Comparing graduates of bachelor's and master's level teacher preparation programs. *The Teacher Educator, 35*(4), 83–96.

Liu, X. S., & Meyer, J. P. (2005). Teachers' perceptions of their jobs: A multilevel analysis of the teacher follow-up survey for 1994–95. *Teachers College Record, 107*(5), 985–1003.

Lortie, D. (1975). *School teacher: A sociological study.* Chicago: University of Chicago Press.

McDonald, F. (1980). *Study of induction programs for beginning teachers (Vol. 1). The problems of beginning teachers. A crisis in training.* Princeton, NJ: Educational Testing Service.

McCann, T. M., & Johannessen, L. R. (2004). Why do new teachers cry? *The Clearing House, 77,* 138–145.

McCann, T. M., Johannessen, L. R., & Ricca, B. (2005). *Supporting beginning English teachers: Research and implications for teacher induction.* Urbana, IL: National Council of Teachers of English.

Merriam, S. B. (1988). *Case study research in education: A qualitative approach.* San Francisco: Jossey-Bass.

Merseth, K. K. (1990). Supporting beginning teachers with computer networks. *Journal of Teacher Education, 42*(2), 140–147.

Myers, M. D. (1997, June). Qualitative research in information systems. *MIS Quarterly, 21*(2), 241–242. [Electronic Version].

Nicholson, S. & Bond, N. (2003). Collaborative reflection and professional community building: An analysis of preservice teachers' use of an electronic discussion board. *Journal of Technology and Teacher Education 11*(2), 259–279.

Noddings, N. (1986). Fidelity in teaching, teacher education, and research for teaching. *Harvard Educational Review, 56*(4), 496–510.

Paulus, T., & Scherff, L. (2005, April). *Providing support for pre-service teachers through computer mediated communication.* Paper presented at the annual meeting of the American Educational Research Association (AERA), Montreal, CA.

Rippon, J. H., & Martin, M. (2006).What makes a good induction supporter? *Teaching and Teacher Education, 22*(1), 84–99.

Rogers, D. L., & Babinski, L. (1999, May). Breaking through isolation with new teacher groups. *Educational Leadership, 38*–40.

Rushton, S. P. (2004). Using narrative inquiry to understand a student-teacher's practical knowledge while teaching in an inner-city school. *The Urban Review, 36*(1), 61–79.

Scherff, L. (2006, February). *Why new teachers come and go—what we can do to help them stay.* Paper presented at the annual meeting of the American Association of Colleges of Teacher Education, San Diego, CA.

Scherff, L. (2008). Disavowed: The stories of two novice teachers. *Teaching and Teacher Education, 24,* 1317–1332.

Scherff, L., & Kaplan, J. (2006). Reality check: A teacher educator returns home. *Studying Teacher Education, 2*(2), 155–167.

Shimoni, S., & Lutan, Z. (in press). The development of professional thinking of first year teachers in digital discourse. In I. Kupferberg & E. Olshtain (Eds.), *Educational discourse.* Mofet Institute.

Singer, N. R., & Zeni, J. (2004). Building bridges: Creating an online conversation community for preservice teachers. *English Education, 37*(1), 30–49.

Smagorinksy, P., Cook, L. S., & Johnson, T. S. (2003). The twisting path of concept development in learning how to teach. *Teachers College Record, 105,* 1399–1456.

Smagorinsky, P. Gibson, N., Bickmore, S. T., Moore, C. P., & Cook, L. S. (2004). Praxis shock: Making the transition from a student-centered university program to the corporate climate of schools. *English Education, 36*(3), 214–245.

Sunderman, G. L., Tracey, C. A., Kim, J., & Orfield, G. (2004). *Listening to teachers: Classroom realities and No Child Left Behind.* Cambridge, MA: The Civil Rights Project at Harvard University.

Sweeny, B. W. (2008). *Leading the teacher induction and mentoring program* (2nd ed). Thousand Oaks, CA: Corwin Press and the National Association of Secondary School Principals.

Wade, S. E., & Fauske, J. R. (2004). Dialogue online: Prospective teachers' discourse strategies in computer-mediated discussions. *Reading Research Quarterly, 39*(2), 134–160.

Whipp, J. L. (2003). Scaffolding critical reflection in online discussions: Helping prospective teachers think deeply about field experiences in urban schools. *Journal of Teacher Education*, 54(4), 321–333.

Van Manen, M. (1990). *Researching lived experience: Human science for an action sensitive pedagogy*. Albany, NY: State University of New York Press.

Veenman, S. (1984). Perceived problems of beginning teachers. *Review of Educational Research, 54*(2), 143–178.

Yin, R. K. (2002). *Case study research, design and methods* (3rd ed.). Newbury Park: Sage.

Breinigsville, PA USA
08 August 2010
243138BV00002B/4/P

5967